GERVASE PHINN'S YORKSHIRE JOURNEY

Gervase Phinn's Yorkshire Journey

Gervase Phinn

with watercolours by Matthew Phinn

First published in 2010 by Dalesman
an imprint of
Country Publications Ltd
The Water Mill, Broughton Hall
Skipton, North Yorkshire BD23 3AG
www.dalesman.co.uk

ISBN 978-1-85568-278-8

Frontispiece: 'The beach at Staithes' by Matthew Phinn.

Typeset in Monotype Dante

Printed in China by Latitude Press Ltd.

Dedication
I should like to thank Mark Whitley, my editor at Dalesman, who has been an exceptionally wise and patient guide throughout.

Contents

Photographic acknowledgements

Ampleforth Abbey & School, pp42-3; Lee Beel, pp29 left, 50-1; Richard Benson, pp86 top, 91 bottom, 101 bottom, 106, 113, 122, 125, 126-7, 132 top, 133 top & bottom, 136 top & bottom; Bettys & Taylors of Harrogate, pp49, 93; Bolton Castle, p81; Dorothy Burrows, pp86, p102 top & bottom; Burton Agnes Hall, pp34-5; Castle Howard, pp52 (courtesy Mike Kipling), 53 (courtesy Mike Kipling); Chris Caeser, p29 right; Trevor Croucher, p90; Alan Curtis, pp23 right, 24 bottom, 26, 28, 32, 33 top; Doncaster Council, pp120, 121; Keith Dungate, p107; English Heritage Photo Library (www.englishheritageprints.com), pp44, 45, 114-5, 118 top & bottom, 119 top & bottom, 124; Ian Grundy, p104 bottom; Deryck Hallam, pp58, 60, 76, 85; Harrogate Borough Council, p48; Andrew Hopkins, pp14-15, 68 top, 70 top & bottom, 77, 89, 93 top, 104 top; Paul Jackson, p91 top; Mike Kipling, pp11, 16, 17 top, 18-19 top, 18, 20 top & bottom, 21, 25, 27, 30 bottom, 41, 59, 66-67, 71 top left, 71 top right, 71 bottom, 79, 88 bottom, 98-99, 100, 105 top; Magna Science Adventure Centre, pp128 top & bottom, 129 top & bottom, 130-1; Kippa Matthews, pp62 top & bottom, 63 left, 63 top right; Paul Miguel, pp88 top, 92; Len Morris CPAGB, p101 top; National Coal Mining Museum, pp109 top & bottom; Chris Pearson, p46; Matthew Phinn, p13; John Potter, pp17 bottom, 25, 26-7 top, 31, 33, 40, 69 bottom, 80, 103, 105 bottom, 123, 135 top & bottom, 137; Colin Raw, pp47, 82-3, 87; Sheffield Theatres, p134 (courtesy Jack Eames); Mark Sunderland, pp61, 84; Rotherham Metropolitan Borough Council, Archives & Local Studies Service, p132 bottom; Waterton Park Hotel, pp108 top & bottom; Richard Watson, pp12, 22, 24 top, 30 top, 78; Mark Whitley, p22 left; York Bar Convent, pp68 bottom (courtesy Rob Maw), 69 top (courtesy Rob Maw); York Mystery Plays, p63 bottom right (courtesy *York Evening Press*); York St Peter's School, pp64 top & bottom, 65 top & bottom.

The publishers would like to acknowledge the help of the following in sourcing illustrations: Tim Brannen, Rotherham Archives & Local Studies Service; Anna Briggs, Burton Agnes Hall; Duncan Brown, English Heritage Images; Pat Chandler & Erica Town, York St Peter's School; Laura Crisp, Bettys & Taylors of Harrogate; Alan Curtis; Jo Dodd, York Bar Convent; Anna Holdsworth, Magna Science Adventure Centre; Graham Holman, Turkish Baths & Health Spa; Rachel Jack & Nicole Hingley, Castle Howard; Jillian Johnson, National Centre for Early Music; Marie Lawton, Doncaster Council; Simon Murphy, Waterton Park Hotel; Aukje Noorman, Ampleforth Abbey & School; Tom Orde-Powlett, Bolton Castle; Chris Pearson, Shandy Hall; Marie Riley, Harrogate Borough Council; Philip Strafford, Sheffield Theatres; Joanne Towndrow, National Coal Mining Museum.

Visitor information

Coast
www.discoveryorkshirecoast.com
Flamborough – www.flamborough-pc.gov.uk
Burton Agnes Hall – www.burtonagnes.com

North Yorkshire
www.northyorkmoors.org.uk
Masham – www.visitmasham.com
Ampleforth Abbey & School – www.ampleforth.org.uk
Rievaulx Abbey – www.english-heritage.org.uk/rievaulx
Shandy Hall – www.shandean.org/shandyhall.html
Harrogate – www.harrogate.gov.uk/harrogate-266
Harrogate Royal Baths – www.harrogate.gov.uk/harrogate-1100
Harrogate, Bettys Tea Rooms – www.bettys.co.uk
Castle Howard – www.castlehoward.co.uk

York
www.visityork.org
Minster – www.yorkminster.org
Mystery Plays – www.yorkmysteryplays.co.uk
St Peter's School – www.st-peters.york.sch.uk
Bar Convent – www.bar-convent.org.uk
Viking Festival – www.yorkfestivals.com

Yorkshire Dales
www.yorkshiredales.org.uk
Bolton Castle – www.boltoncastle.co.uk

West Yorkshire
Saltaire – www.saltairevillage.info, www.saltsmill.org.uk
Kirkstall Abbey – www.leeds.gov.uk/kirkstallabbey
Leeds – www.leedsliveitloveit.com
Wakefield – www.wakefield.gov.uk
Walton Hall – www.watertonparkhotel.co.uk
National Coal Mining Museum – www.ncm.org.uk

South Yorkshire
Brodsworth Hall – www.english-heritage.org.uk/brodsworth
Cusworth Hall – www.doncaster.gov.uk
Conisbrough Castle – www.conisbroughcastle.org.uk
Roche Abbey – www.english-heritage.org.uk/roche_abbey
Magna – www.visitmagna.co.uk
Boston Castle & Clifton Park – www.rotherham.gov.uk
Sheffield Lyceum – www.sheffieldtheatres.co.uk
Rotherham Minster – www.rotherhamminster.org

Introduction

Glancing through this book and seeing the places represented within, the reader might be rather puzzled. Of all the locations in this great county of Yorkshire — the stunning dales and the bleak moors, the grand houses and impressive castles, the towering minsters and quaint villages, the crashing waterfalls and outstanding scenery — why has the author, you might ask, composed such an apparently random selection?

Well, *Gervase Phinn's Yorkshire Journey* is indeed idiosyncratic, but the selection is not an arbitrary one. It represents a personal tour of places and buildings which have meant a great deal to me, for the abbeys and churches, castles and museums, parks and holiday resorts in a sense define my childhood. To me they are very special places, some of which are little known and rarely visited. Their story deserves to be told.

I was born in Rotherham, viewed in the popular mind as a dark, depressing, brooding, Northern industrial place with little to commend it. The gloomy image of this industrial town in the Don Valley, a place of dust and dirt, of noisy steelworks (where my father worked) and ugly pitheads, was not wholly true. There were, of course, the smoky mornings, impenetrable smog and an unpleasant odour which sometimes emanated from the canal and the river, but a bus ride out of the centre of the town took you in minutes into open country.

Such beauty so close to heavy industry still comes as a great surprise to visitors to the area. Over the past two or three

decades the landscape has undergone massive changes for the better. Heavy industry has declined, fish have returned to the rivers Don and Rother, and along the riverbanks willows grow and shrubs flourish. The steelworks where my father worked most of his life has been turned into a magnificent museum.

In the school holidays I would explore the area around the town. I would set off in the morning on my bike with a bottle of pop and a sandwich, and cycle out of Rotherham and into the country, returning only when it began to get dark.

One of my favourite destinations was Roche Abbey. I would cycle out to Wickersley, famous for the grindstones used in the Sheffield cutlery trade, through the mining town of Maltby and into the open country, eventually arriving at the crumbling remains of the magnificent Cistercian abbey.

After I had read Sir Walter Scott's epic story *Ivanhoe*, I cycled out one bright Saturday morning to Conisbrough Castle, near Doncaster, where the novel is set. I recall sitting on the perimeter wall staring up at the imposing edifice and imagining knights in glittering armour, gallant Crusaders, dastardly villains, jousting and sieges, dark dungeons and great battles.

Other places of interest around the town to which I would cycle included: Cusworth Hall, which now houses the museum of South Yorkshire; Keppel's Column, a towering pillar with a viewing platform at the top, erected in 1778 by the second Marquess of Rockingham to commemorate the acquittal of his friend Admiral Keppel; Hoober Stand, a strange triangular and tapering 518-foot (158 m) high structure with a hexagonal lantern and built in 1748 to celebrate the victory of the Duke of Cumberland at Culloden Moor in 1746; and the Needle's Eye, a bizarre folly dating from 1780 and sited at the edge of Lee Wood on the Wentworth Woodhouse estate. The Needle's Eye is a strange triangle of stone with a huge urn on the pinnacle and a gateway through the centre.

The town centre of Rotherham was and still is dominated by the great red sandstone church of All Saints with its magnificent 180-foot (55 m) spire. Built in the thirteenth century, it is one of the finest examples of Perpendicular architecture in Yorkshire. A walk away is the Bridge Chapel of Our Lady, a rare survivor of mediaeval times.

facing page:
'Tickhill in winter' by Matthew Phinn.

As a teenager I was rather different from boys my age in finding such old stone structures — castles and churches, follies and abbeys — of interest but the stories behind such buildings fascinated me. I still feel a thrill when standing on a battlement or amidst the ruins of an abbey or in a great cathedral, imagining times past.

Of course I didn't spend all my time searching for ruins and visiting churches and monuments. Other destinations for me were Elsecar Reservoir, Worsborough Dam, Sprotborough Canal, Swinton Lock, and the 'hell hole' (a dark and sinister stretch of water) at Whiston Meadows. I would visit the surrounding villages of Hooten Roberts, Firbeck, Tickill, Laughton, Letwell, Thorpe Salvin and Wentworth, all with their own distinctive characters and set amongst open country. Tickhill with its duck pond, buttercross, crumbling castle and magnificent St Mary's Church was my favourite, and I spent many a happy hour fishing for minnows in the stream.

There are two parks in Rotherham, and both were favourite haunts of children in the 1950s and '60s. Clifton Park on the corner of Clifton Lane and Doncaster Road was created to serve the leisure needs of a growing population. I preferred Boston Park. There were fewer park keepers hovering around to tell children to keep to the path, and more space and freedom. At the entrance stood a small squat building, Boston Castle, with battlements and small square mullioned windows, erected as a hunting lodge by the Earl of Effingham who originally owned the land.

My parents were great day-trippers and most weekends found us — Mum and Dad, my two brothers and sister and myself — in a green Morris Oxford heading for the coast.

As we sped along on our trip to the seaside, Dad would be full of fanciful tales. On the way we always passed under a low bridge and Dad would tell us about the driver of a double-decker bus who, misjudging the height, sheered off the top of the vehicle. "And every single passenger on the bus was decapitated," he told us. On the way home in the shadowy darkness we would pass over a small hump-backed bridge. As we approached he would tell us of the great, green, hairy monster which lived beneath with its dripping fangs and red-rimmed eyes. He would slow down and nearly stop at the brow of the hill and announce in a mock-frightened voice, "We've broken down." We would all howl.

Once at the seaside (usually Bridlington) we made straight for the ice-cream parlour and, if the sea was calm, we headed for the quay for a trip around the bay on the *Yorkshire Belle*. Another of Dad's stories was how the leaking vessel had sailed to Dunkirk to rescue the stranded British troops. I have an idea that this particular story was true.

If it was Filey it would be a stroll along the Brigg followed by fish and chips, smothered in salt and vinegar, eaten out of newspaper as we sat on the harbour wall.

Sometimes we would go further afield: to Staithes, where time seemed to have stopped; Sandsend, where we would search for fossils and walk along the great stretch of golden sand; Robin Hood's Bay, where we would explore the narrow entries; Runswick Bay, where the cluster of cottages seemed to cling precariously to the cliffside; and, of course, Whitby with its quaint streets, picturesque quay and imposing abbey.

Scarborough was another favourite destination. I loved making sandcastles on the soft sandy beach, the donkey rides, steering the little motor boats on the boating lake, listening to the music at the Spa, and walking along the promenade, lips sticky from candy floss and the sweet pink sticks of rock which lasted for hours and hours. I loved the climb up to the castle and later, hungry from the walk, fish and chips with bread and butter and a pot of tea in the café on the front.

Until the sixth form I had seen very little of Yorkshire, but at seventeen was introduced to the dales and the moors by an inspirational geography master, J Alan Taylor. 'J A T' clearly loved his subject and taught us with such enthusiasm and rigour, believing that geography was best studied in the field — "first-hand experience" was his favourite catchphrase. He organised many a field trip at weekends, during the school holidays and for a week out of school at the end of each term. These were eagerly anticipated, especially since we joined up with the girls from the girls' high school, under the watchful eye of Mrs Taylor, who was head of the geography department in the girls' school.

One memorable field trip was to Malham Cove. We had read about 'clints' and 'grykes', limestone pavements and caverns, potholes and subterranean rivers in our physical geography textbook. I was not prepared, however, for what I was to see. We approached by a footpath from the south, and this immense bow-shaped cove came into view like some great walled cathedral. It was breathtaking. I had never seen anything quite as bleak and rugged. Mr Taylor had us stand beneath the towering cove and not say anything at all — just take it in for a moment. Then he explained that it was formed millions of years ago when the earth's crust cracked, fracturing the rock so that it dropped vertically.

"It's over two hundred feet high," he told us, "and a thousand feet wide, and once a crashing waterfall cascaded over the vertical cliff, creating a fall higher than the Niagara Falls. Now can your small minds take that in?"

That week we spent at the youth hostel in the ancient village of Malham, and saw bubbling springs and crashing cataracts, crags and scars, ravines and overhanging cliffs and the dramatic Malham Tarn, one of the two natural lakes in the Yorkshire Dales.

I discovered the North York Moors on another of Mr Taylor's expeditions. This silent and bleak world with its great tracts of heather and bracken fascinated me. We stayed in youth hostels and explored the surrounding landscape, visited great abbeys like Byland and Rievaulx, ate our sandwiches in the shadow of lofty castles at Helmsley and Pickering, and sat in the sunshine outside local inns in villages untouched by modern life. One weekend Mr Taylor led us deep within the North York Moors towards the coast at Ravenscar.

Then there was Boggle Hole. We stayed in the youth hostel, a converted mill set in the hillside and within a stone's throw of the sea, and we explored the streams and woods, the beach and the smugglers' cave. Years later I was to take a party of children for a week to Boggle Hole and we wrote stories about the hob-goblins, those mischievous sprites, which lived thereabouts.

When I was in the sixth form I joined a group of girls and their teachers from Notre Dame Convent in Sheffield where my sister taught, and we travelled to York, a city I had never visited. The city walls, Clifford's Tower, the ancient buildings, towering Minster, cobbled alleyways and narrow streets fascinated me. It was a world away from Rotherham. We were there to watch a cycle in the York Mystery Plays, an experience never to be forgotten. The girls had to leave early to catch the last train, but I was so captivated I stayed on and spent the night sleeping on a bench in York Station. It was worth it.

Following sixth form it was college in Leeds and then a teaching career in Rotherham, Doncaster and Sheffield.

Finally I spent ten memorable years as a school inspector in North Yorkshire, based in the beautiful spa town of Harrogate. During that time, travelling from school to school, I came to know 'God's own country' well and to appreciate its infinite variety. I still marvel at the beauty of Swaledale; I still feel a thrill as I stand on the chalk clifftop at Flamborough Head; I still feel that sense of awe and wonder at the sight of the cold grey fells, thick bracken slopes and long belts of dark woodland that stretch to the distant purple peaks. For me, Yorkshire is incomparable.

Coast

facing page:
'Boats at Staithes' by Matthew Phinn.

When, during the summer months, my father was not 'on weekends' at Steel, Peech and Tozer, he would take the family to the East Coast for the day.

As soon as we were in the car leaving Rotherham, the anticipation and excitement grew. There were three favoured resorts: Bridlington, Scarborough and Whitby, all with their own distinctive character and all interesting for a young boy, but Bridlington was my favourite. It seemed brighter, brasher, more lively and colourful than the other two places and there were more things for a youngster to do.

Attired in long khaki shorts, white cotton cap and sandals and wearing cheap plastic sunglasses and with my Brownie box camera around my neck on a string, I would walk with Dad and my brother Alec along the promenade.

"Smell the ozone," Dad would say, breathing in deeply.

If the tide was out he would sit in a deckchair on the beach to read his paper, keeping a wary eye on the two boys as we ran into the sea. I remember vividly the swimming trunks I wore: a dark green, tight-fitting knitted affair with a canvas belt and metal clasp which took some skill to keep on once sodden with water. There is a family photograph of me with my brother, arms around each other, shivering near the sea's edge. We had just emerged from the water and stand there in these heavy, sagging, uncomfortable outfits.

After our swim we would build the most architecturally complex sandcastles, equipped for the task with brightly coloured metal spades with long wooden handles. Mine was blue, Alec's red. We also had substantial metal buckets and a set each of little paper national flags to stick on our creations.

The amusement arcade drew us children towards it like a magnet. We spent our pennies on the old slot machines or to manipulate a large metal claw in a glass case to try and grab a fluffy toy. I, being a Yorkshireman at heart, didn't waste my money on the Laughing Policeman but would wait until somebody else spent a penny. In a glass case was a large puppet of a policeman who came to life, rocking from from side to side and accompanied by a recording of uproarious laughter. It was infectious and a crowd would gather around and just start laughing. You couldn't help it.

Scarborough always seemed to me a bit 'posher' than Brid. It was hilly as well and there were too many manicured gardens and large groups of old people wandering about. And there were not as many amusements.

Quite a lot of the time my brother Alec and I made our own entertainment at the oily brown square of water fancifully called the boating lake. For a shilling my brother and I would, for half an hour, take it in turns to steer a noisy little boat around and around until the man in charge shouted out, "Come in Number Four."

The boating lake was also a good place to go crabbing. We would beg a few bits of bacon rind from the butcher when Mum bought the pork pies for lunch, and spend hours with a length of string and a couple of buckets, seeing which one of us could catch the most crabs. We dangled our string down into the murky water and waited for the gentle tug which signified we had a catch. The trick in getting the crabs in the bucket was to pull on the string really slowly. The crab would dangle by one pincer and be pulled in slowly and carefully. They were usually only small catches, but occasionally Alec would manage to land a big one. People would then crowd round. My brother was an expert at prizing off the crab which clung on tenaciously to the bacon rind. He would grasp the crab with thumb and finger behind the front pincers and pop it in the bucket.

Whitby was very different from the other resorts, and as I grew older it cast its spell and replaced Bridlington in my

Sticky treats at the seaside … the John Bull rock shop at Bridlington.

affections. It was an altogether quieter, rather sleepy, more mysterious place, almost magical with its ruined abbey high on the clifftop.

For an impressionable teenager and an avid reader of adventure stories about pirates, smugglers and daring explorers, the town came to hold a fascination for me. From here whaling ships left port for Greenland, Captain James Cook served his apprenticeship, there were fossils embedded in the rocks, and slivers of jet and amber pebbles to find amongst the rocks.

And, of course, there was Count Dracula. I knew all about the vampire because my brothers delighted in frightening me with stories of Dracula's bloody exploits.

On one visit to the town we climbed up the Church Stairs to the abbey situated high on the clifftop. Dad and Mum told us there was a magnificent view over the harbour from the church, and we could see the famous box pews and the three-decker pulpit. We were deeply unimpressed until Dad mentioned Count Dracula. One hundred and ninety-nine steps later, we arrived at the church but were not overly interested in the famous box pews and three-decker pulpit. We were in search of the vampire. When the vicar, a tall, thin, white-faced individual in a flowing black cape, appeared at the door of the church, I was very impressed.

"Are you Count Dracula?" I asked innocently.

My red-faced parents hurried their little boy down the steps and back to the car.

The old whaling port of Whitby, on the mouth of the River Esk, spreads up the steep sides of the narrow valley carved out by the river's course. Whitby, meaning 'white settlement' in Old Norse, has rarely changed over the years and still retains its charm and its distinctive character.

As a child I loved the walk along the beach to Sandsend searching for fossils and bits of jet. I liked the fishing trips, the visit to see the huge ammonite fossil and perfectly preserved pterodactyl skeleton in the museum, the little bookshop down the narrow street and, of course, the fish and chips eaten as we sat on the harbour wall. I was not that keen, however, on climbing the 199 steps to the abbey, a pilgrimage insisted on by my parents.

Whitby plays host to one of most popular Gothic events in the world. The Gothic Weekend is a twice-yearly festival, first held in the town in 1974. Whitby was chosen in part because of the Dracula connection. Here a group of good-humoured and beautifully attired Goths pose for a photograph in the grounds of the abbey.

"Whitby is rather a fine place," wrote Tennyson, "a river running into the sea between precipices … a gaunt old abbey and older parish church hanging out over the town and hundreds of white gravestones that looked, to my eye, something like clothes laid out to dry."

Here a lone figure wanders amongst the gravestones, with the abbey, sombre and brooding, silhouetted on the clifftop.

Pages 14-15 following:
Oswy (or Oswiu), the Christian king of Northumbria, founded the great abbey at Whitby in AD 656. Under its first abbess, Hilda, Whitby became the centre of learning and literature. Caedmon, reputed to be the first English poet whose identity we know for certain, wrote *The Song of Creation*, one of the earliest and finest examples of Anglo-Saxon literature.

Staithes, pronounced 'Steers' by the locals, is situated on a rugged patch of coastline North of Whitby, tucked into a cleft of rock which forms a natural harbour. This tiny unspoilt village, where Captain Cook was born and raised, has been famous through the centuries for its maritime heritage and was once one of the country's six biggest fishing ports as well as a renowned boat building centre.

Its setting has inevitably attracted many writers and painters over the years, and the Staithes Group of artists was based here in the late 1800s, their work typifying the best in British Impressionist painting. This artistic tradition is continued by modern-day artists like my son Matthew, who painted the eyecatching watercolour on page 8; and Andy Hawkins (pictured above), who studied art at Doncaster and now runs the Hawkins Gallery in Saltburn-by-the-Sea.

"It lay compact in a ravine whose north-east side was the protecting sea cliffs, and its cottages were so closely packed together the tiled roofs were almost continuous, making a great blotch of red slightly varied by a pearly haze of smoke."

Robin Hood's Bay has changed little since Leo Walmsley wrote this over half a century ago. There is a timeless quality here in this remote and uncommercialised village of tightly packed alleys and small cottages.

Robin Hood's Bay is best avoided in summer when an influx of visitors flock down the steep bank and the cobbled slipway to fill the small crescent of sand and shingle. Instead, visit in winter when the village is atmospheric; there is a ghostliness in the deserted alleys and empty cottages.

Millions of years ago, the land upon which Robin Hood's Bay is situated was once a deep ocean rich in sea creatures. In time these marine animals were buried in the mud, and became fossilised. This coast provides one of the best sources in Britain for the fossil hunter and it was on this beach that Glen Jenkinson found the giant ammonite. We were on a sixth form geography field study trip. Glen, much to everyone's annoyance, repeatedly threw huge pebbles into the sea, causing great explosions of water and drenching us, until Mr Taylor, our geography master, told him to desist. Glen dropped the large pebble he was holding. It cracked open to reveal a large and perfectly formed ammonite, which was taken back to school and displayed in the geology room.

Boggle Hole, a picturesque inlet on the East Coast with sweeping views of Robin Hood's Bay, is the setting for one of my stories. I agree with fellow writer, G P Taylor, author of *Shadowmancer* and *Wormwood*, who describes this part of the coast as 'a hidden gem'.

In the youth hostel, a former mill nestling by a beck in a secluded wooded ravine (pictured left), I spent a creative writing weekend with a party of schoolchildren. We searched for fossils, investigated the rock pools, explored the cave where smugglers reputedly hid their contraband and walked part of the Cleveland Way to Whitby before settling down to write our stories. The looming cliffs, the ragged rocks, the stretch of sandy beach, the great grey ocean, the very atmosphere inspired us all.

That same weekend I was told by the warden of the youth hostel:

"You only see them, and then very rarely, if you believe in them."

He was referring, of course, to the mischievous 'little people' who live along the coast and in the more remote corners of the North York Moors. These are the 'boggles', the hobgoblins or friendly spirits who, by day, hide away in the woods and caves but at night, when the moon is high and the tide is out, dance and play on the beach.

What was the writer Tobias Smollett (1721-71) thinking of when he described Scarborough in his novel *Humphrey Clinker* as "a paltry town"? Yorkshire's most famous holiday resort has just about everything to interest and excite the visitor: great scenic beauty, magnificent sandy beaches, a Victorian theatre, a wonderfully varied seafront, an impressive twelfth-century Norman castle (albeit in ruins), unusual churches, a mediaeval harbour (pictured right), fine promenades, busy streets and walled gardens. What more could one want?

Scarborough's impressive Norman castle dominates the headland dividing the north and south bays. Built at the very edge of a 300-foot (90 m) cliff, it is a naturally defended area, practically impregnable and a perfect look-out spot. Not surprisingly, the fortress survived sieges and wars, and suffered serious damage only twice throughout its long history: once during the English Civil War when it was subjected to prolonged cannon fire and again in 1914 when it was bombarded by German battle cruisers.

Scarborough is reputedly England's oldest holiday resort. Its popularity began in the early 1600s, when Mrs Farrow discovered a stream of mineral water flowing from a cliff to the south of the town. The rich and the famous descended on Scarborough to sample the health-giving waters and enjoy the fresh, bracing sea air. In the eighteenth century many new hotels were built to accommodate the ever-increasing number of visitors and the arrival of the railway in the 1850s made Scarborough more accessible.

In 1867 the magnificent Grand Hotel (pictured) was built, which at the time was the largest hotel in the world. I remember one holiday I stood with my father outside the entrance of the palatial Grand. We marvelled at the Gothic splendour: cast-iron balconies, corner domes with porthole windows, the red and orange terracotta, and the great Corinthian columns.

"When I win the football pools," I remember my father saying, "we will all stay here."

Sadly, that was never to be.

The Brontë family had strong associations with Scarborough and made frequent visits to the spa town. Charlotte was so moved by her first view of the sea that she began to cry.

She wrote: "The idea of seeing the sea—of being near it—watching its changes by sunrise, sunset, moonlight and noon-day—in calm, perhaps in storm—fills and satisfies my mind."

This well-maintained gravestone, in the churchyard of St Mary's Parish Church, Scarborough, marks the last resting place of Anne, Charlotte's younger sister and the author of *Agnes Grey* and *The Tenant of Wildfell Hall*. Anne died on the 28th May 1849, aged just twenty-nine (and not twenty-eight as inscribed on the gravestone). Terminally ill with consumption, she travelled to Scarborough with her sister to look at the sea for the last time. Anne's dying words were: "Take courage, Charlotte, take courage."

It was only when my son Matthew was studying for a fine art degree at Leeds University that I discovered in Scarborough this jewel of a building that is the Church of St Martin's-on-the-Hill.

Behind the unprepossessing Victorian façade is a quite magnificent interior. The church was designed by the architect George Frederick Bodley, who became one of the most distinguished architects of his day. Pictured above is the altar and reredos designed by Bodley.

The painted panels, decorative work and stained glass were overseen by William Morris, who commissioned the greatest of the Pre-Raphaelite artists and craftsmen — Dante Gabriel Rossetti, Philip Webb, Edward Burne-Jones and Ford Maddox Brown — to create an elaborate and striking interior.

As a child, Peasholm Park appeared altogether grander than the parks I was used to in Rotherham. There were unusual oriental statues and ornaments, exotic flowers and shrubs, a tree-lined valley with a stream, and a pagoda and cascade on an island (pictured top). Peasholm Park was a tranquil place, well away from the noise and bustle, the amusement arcades and bingo halls of the town, where the family would spend a quiet Sunday afternoon. I recall stretching out on the grass with a book — *Ivanhoe* or maybe the Arthurian Legends — struggling with the words as the light began to fade, forgetting all that was around me and escaping into an adventure where brave knights jousted and fought pitched battles before great towering castles. I had such a glow of well-being.

The tranquility was only disturbed by the 'Battle of Peasholm' (pictured above), which has been fought on the lake by replica ships for more than eighty years.

The beach at Scarborough is one of the finest in Britain. Honey-coloured sand stretches in a vast crescent from towering cliff to towering cliff. What a treat to sit in the sunshine taking in the view or to make sandcastles beneath a summer sky.

Lying on the south side of Filey Bay on the Yorkshire coast is Filey Brigg (pictured above and right), a natural rock promontory with panoramic views of Filey (pictured far right). Filey probably had a central role as a Roman naval base, for a signal station was built on the Brigg in the fourth century AD during the final days of the Roman occupation of Britain.

One memory of Filey sticks like a burr. Dominic, son number three and eight at the time, was walking barefoot across the sands and suddenly began screaming. He had trodden on a weaver fish and the poisonous spines had embedded themselves in his foot. We spent most of the day at Scarborough Hospital.

Walking along the cliffs in winter with a mountainous sea crashing against the white cliffs, one can appreciate how the stretch of the East Coast around Thornwick Bay (pictured left) was a graveyard for seafaring vessels.

What is believed to be the original lighthouse (pictured above) was built in 1806 by a local customs officer to warn of the dangers of the treacherous coast (174 ships had foundered off Flamborough Head in the previous thirty-six years). The present lighthouse, a towering ninety-two feet (28 m) high and with over 3.5 million candle-power, is visible from the sea for some twenty-one miles (34 km). The light can be seen at Scarborough, and as far as Whitby to the north and the River Humber to the south.

My parents retired to Flamborough so I came to know this stunning stretch of the East Coast well.

Situated between Filey and Bridlington, Flamborough, like Scarborough, has two bays: South Landing and North Landing (pictured left). The village itself is situated between the two. The name Flamborough is said to derive from the Anglo-Saxon word *flaen*, meaning 'arrowhead', to reflect the way the promontory thrusts out to the sea.

The village is steeped in local customs, from its traditional knitting patterns for fishermen's jumpers to its Danish sword-dancing

How I loved going to Bridlington as a child. The first stop would be the ice-cream parlour on the front where dad would treat Alec and me to a knickerbocker glory. If the sea was calm we would board the *Yorkshire Belle* for a trip around the harbour (pictured left). Then we bought buckets and spades, built sandcastles on the beach (pictured above) and took a quick dip in the sea.

Before we went home it was a ride on the donkeys (facing page). Alec always seemed to have the placid one which trotted obediently across the sands; I usually ended up with the stubborn donkey called Mabel which wouldn't move, or the lively one called Enoch which galloped off with me holding on for dear life.

Little remains now of the priory founded in Bridlington in the twelfth century by Walter de Gant, lord of the manor of Hunmanby. Built on the site of a Saxon church, the monastery was one of the earliest, largest and richest Augustinian houses in the country. When complete, the building was over 400 feet (120 m) long and 75 feet (23 m) wide, with transepts 150 feet (45 m) long and a magnificent tower.

Kings and pilgrims came to worship here, for it housed the remains to St John of Bridlington, the saintly prior canonized in 1401.

One king, Henry VIII, was no pilgrim and, with the Dissolution of the Monasteries, the priory was virtually destroyed. Lead from the roof was melted down, much of the stonework was used to repair local houses and the harbour, eight tons of silver plate was removed and the venerated shrine of St John burned in the market place; only the nave survived, to serve as the parish church of St Mary (pictured).

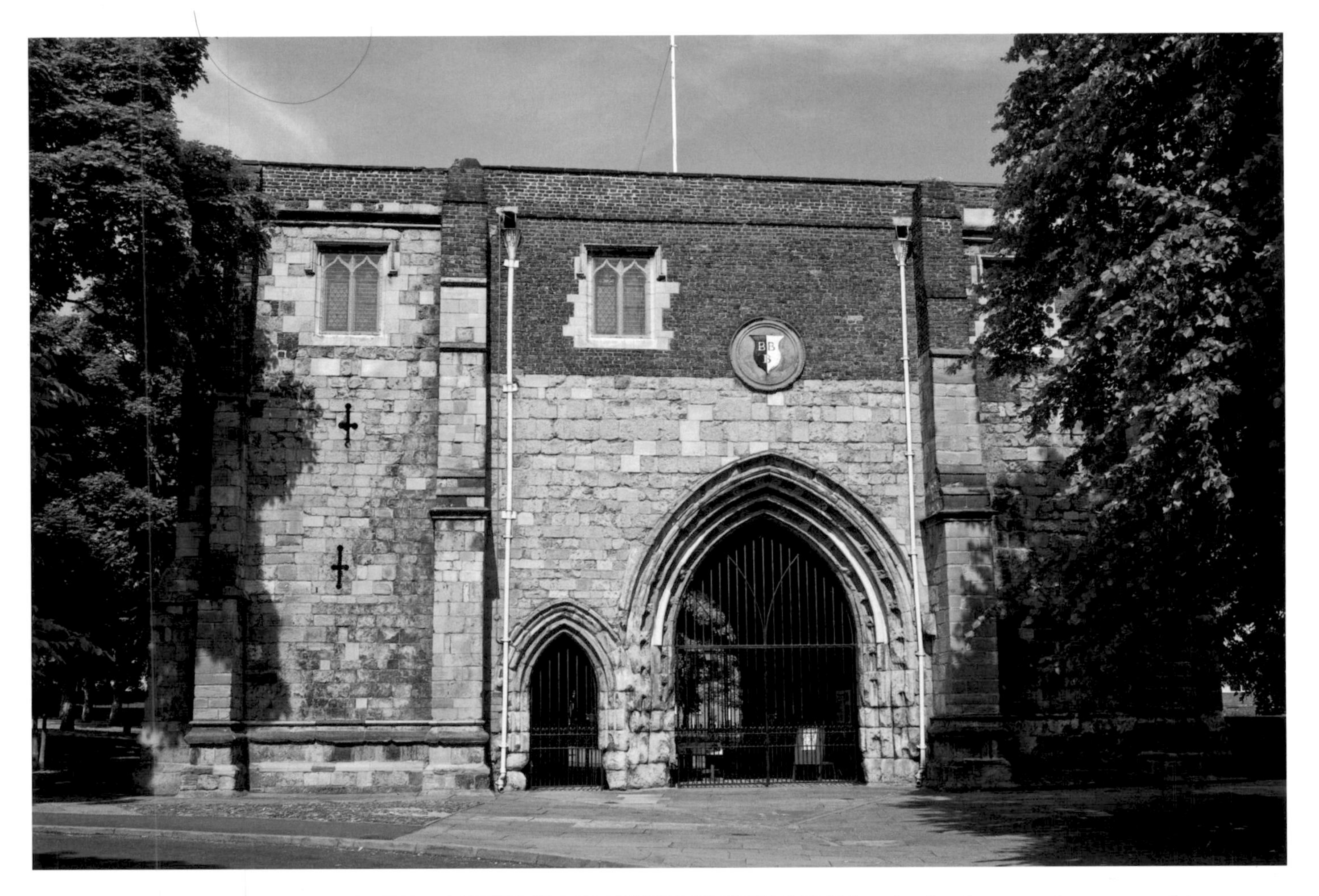

In the fourteenth century, this magnificent building (pictured above) known as the Bayle was the gatehouse to Bridlington Priory. A porter lived here, and monitored the comings and goings of visitors. Over the years the Bayle has been used for many purposes including a prison, courtroom, school and garrison.

Sometimes on our day trip to Bridlington my parents would take the family to Sewerby Hall (pictured above), a fine Georgian house situated on the northern boundary of the town. First it was a visit to view the collection of Amy Johnson memorabilia which is housed here, then (less interesting for a young boy) it was a walk around part of the fifty acres (20 ha) of landscaped gardens; finally we settled on the grass at the clifftop, with its breathtaking views across Bridlington Bay, for a picnic.

I got my first real glimpse of a world of unimaginable privilege when, as a child, I was taken to Burton Agnes Hall (facing page top). This is a grand Elizabethan house with ornate formal gardens (facing page bottom).

The interior (pictured above) was full of treasures: intricate plasterwork ceilings, elaborate wood carvings, fine pieces of porcelain and furniture, and great oil paintings .

What fascinated me most about the house was not the sumptuous interior but the legend. It is said that many years ago the young daughter of the owner, Sir Henry Griffith, was fatally attacked. Before dying she begged her sisters to cut off her head after she died and preserve the skull in the hall which she so loved. The skull remains there still — as reputedly does the ghost of the poor unfortunate girl.

North Yorkshire

I visited Harrogate with my mother when I was fifteen. This impressive spa town was an altogether grander place than Rotherham — elegant, genteel, rather full-of-its-own-importance. On his visit to Harrogate in 1858, Charles Dickens described the town as "the queerest place, with the strangest people in it, leading the oddest lives". Here was opulence on a grand scale. There were wide tree-lined streets, impressive Georgian mansions, luxurious hotels, majestic churches, expensive antique shops, fields and parks, and the famous Royal Baths and Pump Room. The discovery of a chalybeate spring in the sixteenth century changed this small, insignificant town into a spa to rival Cheltenham and Tunbridge Wells. The fame of its healing waters spread, and soon the rich and fashionable were flocking to Harrogate to 'take the waters'.

facing page:
'The North York Moors' by Matthew Phinn.

We had afternoon tea at Bettys Tea Room on Parliament Street. It was the most elegant place I had ever been to. Everything was bright and clean and stylish. We waited in a queue until we were shown to a corner table covered in a spotless and stiff white cloth, and set out with delicate china cups, saucers and plates and heavy silver cutlery. In the centre was a single flower in a small glass vase.

A man sat at a grand piano playing classical music, smiling waitresses in pristine white blouses and starched aprons and dainty caps moved serenely from table to table, and refined people drank from their china cups and dabbed the corners of their mouths with pure white napkins. Tea was dispensed from a heavy silver teapot and a tiered set of sparkling white plates arranged with delicate wafer-thin cucumber and salmon finger sandwiches, tiny iced cakes, butterfly buns, squares of heavy fruit cake, meringues and custard tarts was placed before us. This, I thought, was heaven.

My redoubtable geography master, J Alan Taylor, introduced me to the dales and the moors of North Yorkshire when I was in the sixth form. His most famous saying was that geography and geology are best studied in the field.

"It's all very well reading about limestone scenery and coastal erosion from a textbook," he would say. "You have to see these things at first hand."

Consequently we spent day trips, weekends and field study weeks studying the subjects at first hand.

As a boy from Rotherham I knew the immediate area in which I lived and I had made the occasional visit to the seaside and had a day out to York and Harrogate, but I had never seen the dales and the moors.

I recall the very first hike I did with Mr Taylor. The journey followed the old Viking route known as the Lyke Wake. Legend has it that the Vikings carried the 'lyke' or corpse across the boggy forty miles (65 km) to the sea, where the body was given up to the waves. With the coming of Christianity, the practice was continued, but it took on a deeper meaning and the walk came to symbolise the journey of the soul towards heaven.

I had never seen such magnificent scenery in my life. Beneath a shining blue sky there stretched a landscape of every conceivable colour: brilliant greens, swaths of red and yellow gorse which blazed like a bonfire, dark hedgerows speckled in pinks and whites, twisted black stumps, striding walls and the grey snake of the road curling upwards to the hills in the far distance. Light the colour of melted butter danced amongst the new leaves of early summer.

I remember, too, another of J A T's trips. We scanned the landscape looking for drumlins, described in our textbook, *Physical Geography* by Horrocks, as "basket-of-eggs scenery". I imagined them to be small hummocks but when I enquired of Mr Taylor where these 'drumlins' were, he threw back his head and laughed, and then informed me that I was standing on one — this huge rounded hill. "First-hand experience," he said. I learnt then that fact can sometimes be as fanciful as fiction for the descriptions in Horrocks seemed to me to bear little relation to the real world.

On one expedition in the heat of midsummer the party of sixth-formers, led by Mr Taylor and his wife, trekked up a lonely moorland hill on the North York Moors, through the soft couch grass and sweet smelling heather. Arriving at the brow we peered down at the panorama before us ... and there on a soft grassy bed was a pair of lovers in a passionate embrace, the sun beating down on their naked limbs. As we were ushered away from the summit by a red-faced Mrs Taylor, one cheeky student (Glen Jenkinson as I recall) asked her husband, "Is that what is meant by first-hand experience, sir?"

When I became a school inspector in North Yorkshire, I visited Ampleforth College. I had been invited by the then headmaster, Father Dominic, to attend a school drama production. I duly arrived in good time and parked my car (an old black Volvo estate) in front of the main building. Two young students, aged about thirteen, dressed in smart sports jackets and flannels, approached me and informed me that, being rather early, I might like to look around the college.

"And how are you finding the Volvo?" asked the one of the boys as we climbed the steps to the abbey.

I explained that, with four young children, it was ideal. It was roomy and comfortable, a little heavy on petrol but very safe and reliable. It was getting on a bit but had a good few miles left in it yet.

The boy, clearly something of an expert on cars, then proceeded to suggest various other vehicles in which I might be interested should I be changing the car.

When I visited the college some years later, I parked my car (a smart new Toyota Avensis) in front of the main building and I climbed out. Two senior students in smart grey suits were walking past. One of them smiled.

"I see you've changed the Volvo, sir," he said, smiling.

Masham has an interesting history. Since the Archbishop of York was unwilling to make the long journey north to oversee the town's affairs, Masham was granted a special status in mediaeval times when the parish was designated a 'peculiar'. This meant it had its own ecclesiastical court and dealt with its own affairs. To this day, the vicar cannot be ordered to attend the archbishop but must be formally invited. The peculiar also lives on in the 'Four and Twenty' — the peculiar court which now has a charitable function — and, of course, in the famous Theakston beer, Old Peculier.

A plaque by the mediaeval market cross commemorates the first market charter granted to Masham in 1250 and has been for many centuries the site for the annual sheep fair. Over 80,000 head of sheep were sold here at one time, including animals from the flocks of nearby Fountains and Jervaulx abbeys. The tradition continues on a smaller scale each September.

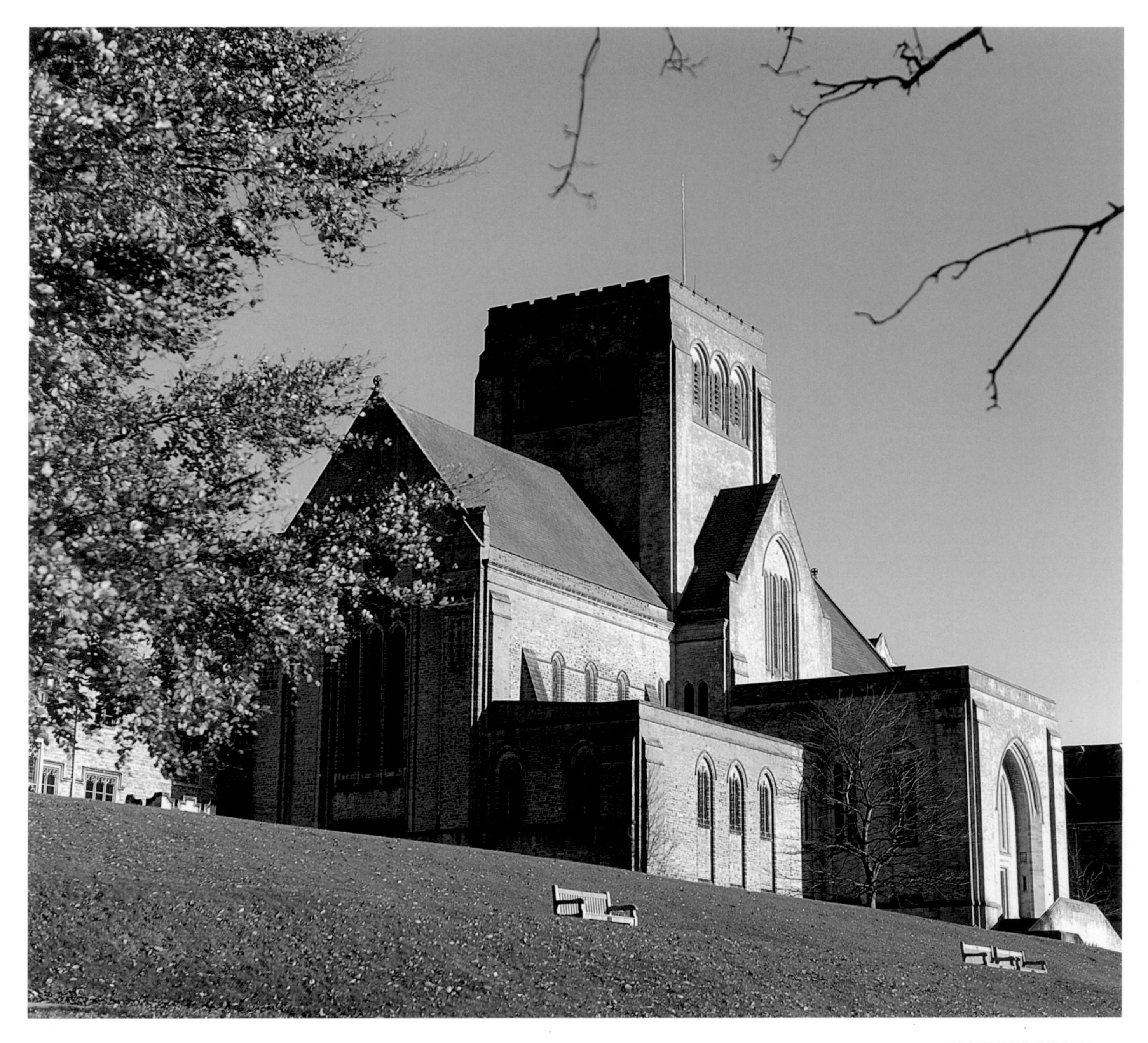

In 1792 the Benedictine order was expelled from France following the French Revolution. Fortuitously one of the priests, Father Anselm Bolton, had come to Ampleforth as the chaplain of Lady Anne Fairfax who lived at Gilling Castle which was just two miles (3 km) away and which is now the site of the preparatory school. Lady Anne built Ampleforth Lodge for her chaplain just before she died, and in 1802 Father Anselm handed the house over to his brethren to be their new monastery (pictured above). In the following year the new monastery school opened.

When I visited Ampleforth College (pictured above) to attend a school drama production, I was greeted by two students who took me on a tour of the college and the abbey. I was given details of the old boys, sporting successes, academic achievements and the excellent facilities.

"The monks didn't settle at Ampleforth until 1802," one student told me, "but the community goes back long before that."

Then the other boy added proudly, "It's the finest abbey in the North and best public school in the country, you know."

In 1919, Father Paul Nevill, a former headmaster of Ampleforth College, asked Robert Thompson, a carpenter and woodcarver who lived near Kilburn, to make the furniture for Ampleforth Abbey (pictured above).

This was Thompson's first commission and his craftsmanship was so admired that Ampleforth requested more work, including the furniture and fittings for the library and most of the main building.

Robert 'Mouseman' Thompson's beautiful oak furniture, inspired by the Arts and Crafts movement led by William Morris, often features a carved mouse somewhere on the piece. It is claimed that the mouse trademark came about accidentally following a conversation about 'being as poor as a church mouse', which took place between Thompson and one of his colleagues during the carving of a cornice for a screen.

In 1132, St Bernard of Clairvaux sent twelve monks from Clairvaux in France to found the abbey of Rievaulx. It took its name from a direct translation of the French meaning 'Rye Vale'. Today the ancient imposing walls are surrounded by manicured lawns, neat copses and long meadows, but when Walter Espec encouraged the group of French monks to build an abbey here, the land was said to be fit for only "wild beasts and robbers".

At the Dissolution of the Monasteries, Rievaulx's new owner, Thomas Manners, first Earl of Rutland and one of Henry VIII's advisers, wasted no time in overseeing the systematic destruction of this magnificent building. Remarkably, some of the impressive architectural treasures have, in part, survived, and serve as reminders of Rievaulx's original splendour. Most of the thirteenth-century presbytery (pictured above), which rises a full three stories in height and shows off Early English flying buttresses, still stands; and the monks' refectory gives an indication of the dimensions of this huge communal hall.

According to the Lonely Planet guidebook, Rievaulx "is everything a ruin should be: battered enough by the passage of time to give it a venerable air, but with enough beautiful stonework, soaring pillars and graceful arches remaining so you can imagine how it looked in its thirteenth-century heyday."

Shandy Hall, in the village of Coxwold, was a mediaeval priest's house which was extended in the seventeenth century, and then 'modernized' by Laurence Sterne, who lived there from 1760 until his death in 1768.

It is now a museum, and houses the largest collection of first and contemporary editions of Sterne's works anywhere in the world. There are also autograph letters, tithe accounts, portraits, contemporary prints and copies of the newspapers to which Sterne contributed.

"I am persuaded that every time a man smiles — but much more so when he laughs — it adds something to this fragment of life."

So wrote the novelist, wit and bon viveur, the Rev Laurence Sterne, who lived in Shandy Hall, a house as architecturally eccentric as its former occupant. Sterne's study is pictured here.

This unconventional character was clearly temperamentally unsuited for the role of a country parson.

My former English teacher, the wonderful Miss Wainwright, would certainly not have approved of Sterne's taste for the high life — wine, gambling, hunting, horse racing, cock fighting and extra-marital affairs — but she considered his picaresque novel *The Life and Opinions of Tristram Shandy, Gentleman* to be one of the comic classics of English literature.

Situated in salubrious Low Harrogate, the Valley Gardens, which, along with woodland known as the Pinewoods, cover seventeen acres (7 ha), contain the greatest number of mineral springs in the town. Beautiful buildings such as the Sun Pavilion, the Colonnades and the Tea Room (pictured above) are located in the midst of this tranquil park. The stunning Sun Pavilion, typical of the Art Deco period, has been the venue of many events and gatherings since the 1930s.

Opened in 1897, Harrogate's Royal Baths (pictured left) were once one of Europe's leading destinations for the rich and the famous. Politicians and royalty were amongst those who came to take the famously sulphurous waters and be invigorated in the Turkish Baths.

The original guidebook has some interesting information for would-be bathers:

"While lying down in the hottest room, the attendant will bring a tumbler of cold water; if not, it should be asked for, or taken from the tap. If there is any fullness in the head, or faintness, the bath man should be summoned by clapping the hands. If the feet are cold, the bath man will douche them with hot water, and some bathers may with advantage have a hot needle bath; indeed, for any disagreeable symptoms the bath man should be consulted, and from his immense experience he will probably know the appropriate remedy."

In 1919 a Swiss confectioner, Frederick Belmont, opened his first Bettys Café Tea Rooms in Harrogate (pictured above and left), which had become one of the country's most fashionable spa towns. The young Frederick originally planned to establish his business in a resort on the South Coast, but the beautiful countryside and clear air of Yorkshire so much reminded him of his native land that he decided to stay.

No visit to Harrogate would be complete without a visit to Bettys, with its combination of an elegant setting, mouth-watering sandwiches and confectionery, and Yorkshire warmth and hospitality.

Pages 50-1 following:
Every journey into the North York Moors is different and every scene has a unique beauty. It was a mild September when I drove across the moors above Rosedale. On such a late summer evening the colouring of the scene was unforgettable: an ocean of bright heather, great rusty-coloured rocks, russet bracken slopes and grey woodsmoke rising to the purple of the sky. It was a vast, beautiful and silent world.

In 1778, a visitor to Castle Howard was startled by the unbalanced appearance and architectural discrepancies of this vast and imposing palace. He observed that the two separate wings "stand staring at each other, as much as to say, 'What business have you here?'."

Designed for Charles Howard, the third Earl of Carlisle, by Sir John Vanbrugh, construction of this flamboyant Baroque pile started in 1700 but with many later additions. It is not to everyone's taste. Indeed the fifth earl recalled how the family found it hard to understand their father's decision to build a new wing "not correspondent to the other, or to the centre part of the house", and that his father too was unhappy with the result, complaining that the house has many "unconquerable faults".

With all its "unconquerable faults", for me, Castle Howard, with its huge crowning dome and sumptuous interiors (pictured right), is an architectural masterpiece.

York

Of all the cities and towns in this country, my very favourite is York. One enters the city, enclosed by almost unbroken walls, through formidable mediaeval gateways to discover magnificent half-timbered buildings like St William's College, fine seventeenth century brick houses such as the Dutch House, elegant Georgian residences and tranquil gardens, narrow streets and snickleways, cobbled yards and Roman columns, ancient towers and battle-scarred parapets — evidence of the city's great and glorious past.

Towering above everything is the mighty Minster: the Metropolitan and Cathedral Church of St Peter, described by the poet Robert Southey as "a monument of magnificent piety".

It was only recently that I learned that York Minster has its own constabulary which dates back to 1275. Sir Robert Peel is said to have examined the Minster Police before forming the British police force. John Key, a police officer at the Minster, sent me a copy of his entertaining collection, *Close Encounters*, which he had written to raise funds for Martin House, Yorkshire's first hospice for children and young people. His book contains a brief history of the Minster police force and some splendid short stories — some hilariously funny, others very poignant — all based on the encounters the author has had with the public on his nightly foot patrols around the great cathedral. He comes across a German student who has set up his tent for the night in the dean's garden, several elderly

facing page:
'York and the Minster' by Matthew Phinn.

gentlemen who decide to consume their fish and chips in the nave, a vagrant who shelters from the rain with his dog, two would-be robbers, a distraught young woman who comes to the cathedral on New Year's Eve and a large American woman who is in desperate search of "the john".

The office of the Minster policeman derives from that of the Constable of the Liberty — a long-established post that was similar to that of the parish constable. In 1285, Minster Close was enclosed by a twelve-foot (3.5 m) wall within which the Dean and Chapter were the law. The Liberty had its own chief constable, constables, coroners, magistrates, bailiffs and stewards.

Times do not appear to have changed a great deal when one reads the records, for two hundred and fifty or so years ago there was even then a deal of 'disturbance' and 'misbehaviour' on a Saturday night. The magistrates sitting at the Hall of Pleas in 1740 issued the following notice:

Whereas grievous disturbances and disorders do frequently happen in the Cathedral church and within its Liberty, also the constables of the said Minster Yard and officers of the said Cathedral are often abused in executing their office and endeavouring to suppress these several disorders aforesaid for the effectual preventing whereof for the future…

It is interesting to reflect on the fact, even then, that cities had their fair share of "grievous disturbances and disorders".

A very proud moment in my life was when, in 2003, an honorary fellowship of St John's College was conferred upon me in York Minster. Since then the college, nationally renowned as a centre of learning, has continued to flourish and become the University of York St John.

I once accompanied a school party around the vast cathedral. The teacher and her class of seven and eight year olds, who had travelled from a tiny village primary school in the heart of the Dales, stood in the centre of the great cathedral. They all stared at the Great East Window, the largest mediaeval stained-glass window in Europe, the size of a double tennis court. They gazed up in wonder at the great arched roof.

"It's awesome, isn't it?" she said. "It's so vast."

"Aye, miss," agreed a little boy from a farming background. "It is that. And I'll tell thee what — it'd mek a champion barn."

When I was asked to speak and present prizes at St Olave's, the junior department of St Peter's, reputedly the oldest school in England, I readily accepted. I had passed the imposing building with its turrets and towers many times, and always wanted to look around inside. Now here was my chance. The portrait in the great hall intrigued me. I knew that bearded face with a large hat pulled rakishly down on his head. "Yes," said the master, "it is Guy Fawkes — one of our old boys." The school, he told me, has a certain affection for their best-known former pupil who was once tactfully described by a head boy at a speech day at the school as "not exactly a role model".

I first visited the Bar Convent, situated just outside the city walls at Micklegate Bar, when I was a student teacher in Leeds. My flatmate was on teaching practice at the convent which then housed a girls' school, and he was intending to accompany the teachers and students to Stratford-on-Avon to see a production of *King Lear* but he was ill. Sister Margaret Mary suggested I might like to take his place. At the time I saw little of the building but years later, when I was asked to become a patron of the Bar Convent Heritage Appeal, I was able to spend a day at this hidden gem. The Bar Convent is the oldest living convent in England, established as a school for Catholic girls in 1686. The community at the Bar Convent belong to the Congregation of Jesus which was founded by the Yorkshire woman, Mary Ward (1585-1645). She was a pioneer of education for women and fought for the right of religious sisters to pursue a variety of ministries outside the convent walls. On the current site is a Grade I listed Georgian building dating back to the 1760s.

The Minster, St Peter's and the Bar Convent are just three of York's treasures. For almost two thousand years the city has been at the very centre of great historical events, and some of England's fiercest and bloodiest battles have been fought on the flat land around, decisive battles like Stamford Bridge, Towton and Marston Moor to name but three. York is steeped in history, and has some of the most imaginative museums in the country. It is a city like no other.

York Minster, pictured above from Lendal Bridge, and the vast interior, right. The largest mediaeval Gothic building in northern Europe, it took about 250 years to build. It replaced a small Anglo-Saxon stone Minster which was ravaged by fire. The Normans decided to build a new Minster on a fresh site to replace the old fire-damaged church and, around the year 1080, Thomas of Bayeux, the new Archbishop of York, decided to have a cathedral built.

The poet, Robert Southey, was overwhelmed by the immensity and beauty of the church, although there is a sting in his adulation:

"The praise must be given to the English heretics that they preserve these monuments of magnificent piety with proper care."

York Minster contains some of the world's most breathtaking stained glass. There are 128 windows in the cathedral, made up of approximately two million individual pieces of glass.

The magnificent Great East Window (pictured above) is the largest example of mediaeval stained glass in the world. Created between 1405 and 1408, it covers approximately 2,100 square feet (195 m²).

The West Window is affectionately known as the 'Heart of Yorkshire' because of the heart shape in its flamboyant tracery.

Another spectacular window is the Five Sisters which contains the largest amount of Early English grisaille glass (painted in grey monochrome to imitate sculpture) in a single window anywhere in the world.

Clifford's Tower, so called after Roger de Clifford who was hanged there in 1322, is a reminder of the horror which took place in 1190. In that year the city's Jewish community took refuge on the wooden keep which was on this site. King Henry II had been careful to protect England's Jews, but with his death and the accession of the crusading King Richard, a number of violent outbursts against Jews took place in various English towns, including York. An incident in the city was quickly followed by most of the Jews seeking protection within the castle. Rather than fall into the hands of the mob, many of the Jews committed suicide and set the keep afire. The survivors emerged the following day, only to be massacred by the besiegers.

In mediaeval York, the Mystery Plays were an expression of civic piety on the feast of Corpus Christi. Held annually on the Thursday after Trinity Sunday, in late May and the middle of June, they presented the 'History of the World' from the mystery of the Creation, through the birth, death and resurrection of Christ, to the Last Judgement. The plays taught a simple message, but not in a simple way. Written to appeal to all sections of the community, they were highly dramatic, sophisticated and often lavishly presented.

Pictured above is the Baptism of Christ from 2002; and right, the Flood from 2000.

Actors who have played Christ include Victor Bannarjee, Robson Green, Christopher Timothy, Simon Ward and, in 2000, Ray Stevenson (pictured above); another famous name to have appeared in the Mystery Plays is York-born Dame Judi Dench, who played the Angel of the Resurrection in 1954 (pictured below).

The York Cycle of Mystery Plays comprises a number of individual pageants and were originally presented by different guilds of craftsmen within the city — which were also known as 'mysteries', hence the name of the plays. The different guilds often performed appropriate stories, so for example the shipwrights were responsible for the Building of the Ark, while the butchers played the Death of Christ.

Using the colourful language of mediaeval Yorkshire, the actors still parade through the streets in wagon teams (pictured above) presenting the great moments of Christian history at twelve playing stations marked by city banners. Although the Mystery Plays were revived in the 1951 York Festival of the Arts, they were performed on a fixed stage in the Museum Gardens; it was not until 1954 that a wagon play was offered in the streets.

The educational historian A F Leach described St Peter's School in York as "Older than the House of Commons, older than the Universities, older than the House of Lords, older even than the throne or the nation itself."

Despite what my wife's cousin contends (that King's School in Canterbury is the oldest school in the country) there is little doubt that St Peter's School, built in AD 627 on the site of the present York Minster, is the more ancient.

There have been a good few tearaway pupils in the past at St Peter's School, even 600 years ago. A fourteenth-century report describes the skirmishes between the boys of St Peter's and bargees on the Ouse, one pupil being carried off on a barge. Some Peterites retaliated by pushing a bargee into the river where he drowned. The headmaster made the boys pay for his funeral. Thankfully the present students at the school are better behaved.

Pages 66-7 following:
I recall the first time I visited York, entering through a formidable mediaeval gateway and into a world of half-timbered buildings, elegant Georgian residences, tranquil gardens, narrow streets, snickleways and cobbled yards, ancient towers and battle-scarred parapets. And towering above was the mighty Minster, the Metropolitan and Cathedral Church of St Peter, York's crowning glory.

The original seventeenth-century house which became the Bar Convent was purchased by Francis Bedingfield in 1686 and replaced in the eighteenth century by the spectacular Georgian building (pictured above) now listed as Grade I by English Heritage.

The building remains the home of the York Community of the Congregation of Jesus, and is open daily for interest, education and enjoyment.

This is one of the county's hidden gems, and houses the most fascinating collection of artefacts, paintings, religious relics, historical documents, a stunning Maw tiled floor (pictured right), winter garden and a priest hole.

The buildings at the Bar Convent include what was once an open courtyard but which is now a splendid Victorian tiled entrance hall (pictured opposite page bottom). There is also the great parlour, the library, and the stunningly beautiful Neoclassical chapel (pictured above) which was hidden from view and completed in secret in 1769 by Thomas Atkinson before the repeal of the Penal Laws for Catholics.

The community at the Bar Convent belong to the Congregation of Jesus which was founded by the Yorkshire woman, Mary Ward (1585-1645), pictured right. During the reign of Queen Elizabeth I and the persecution of Roman Catholics, it was a secret community known as the 'Ladies at the Bar'. The sisters wore plain grey day dresses rather than habits to avoid arousing suspicion.

The museum tells the story of how the sisters lived and worked in secrecy to preserve their way of life in times of terrible persecution, as well as the lack of recognition of the value of education for girls and women and the contribution they could make to society.

The Clitherow home, located in a small mediaeval house at 10 the Shambles, became a place of refuge for fugitive priests at the time of Elizabeth I. In 1586, on the discovery of a secret cupboard with vestments, wine and bread for mass, as well as a 'priest's hole', Margaret Clitherow was arrested and tried. At her trial when she was asked for her plea, she replied:

"I know of no offence whereof I should confess myself guilty. Having made no offence, I need no trial."

The penalty for refusing to plea was extremely harsh but she refused to allow a trial at which her children would be forced to testify against her. Because Margaret Clitherow refused to stand trial, the penalty was death by crushing. She was told:

"You must return from whence you came, and there, in the lowest part of the prison, be stripped naked, laid down, your back on the ground, and as much weight laid upon you as you are able to bear, and so to continue for three days without meat or drink, and on the third day to be pressed to death, your hands and feet tied to posts, and a sharp stone under your back."

Ten days later, the sentence was carried out. A board was placed on her and huge stones were laid on top. She was dead within fifteen minutes.

Her shrine consists of a single small room in the house in which she once lived. A plaque on the wall (pictured above) explains Margaret's story, and there are statues of her and a priest behind an altar (picured top).

York — ancient port, garrison town, and ecclesiastical and administrative centre — is steeped in history, and has some of the most imaginative and innovative pageants, exhibitions and festivals in the country. These include the Viking Festival held in February, where great bearded men and flame-haired maidens invade the city once again.

Yorkshire Dales

JB Priestley, who chose to have his ashes laid to rest in the small church at Hubberholme, said: "On all my travels I've never seen a countryside to equal the beauty of the Yorkshire Dales."

The scenery in this part of England is indeed striking, and includes some of the most varied and stunning landscapes in the British Isles. The county may not embrace within its sprawling borders the vast magnificence of the Scottish Highlands or the towering grandeur of Snowdonia but there is a particular appeal in each of the diverse landscapes. There is a breathtaking beauty in the hay meadows of Wensleydale and Swaledale, and there is a simple pastoral beauty in the close-cropped sheep pastures of Ribblesdale. This is a land of contrasts: of dark, scattered woodland, soaring fellsides leading to vast empty moors, wind-scoured crags, bubbling becks, and vast swathes of crimson heather and golden bracken.

With each season this vast landscape changes dramatically but it is in winter that the most spectacular transformation takes place. It is then that the multicoloured canvas of pale green fields and dark fells is enveloped in one endless white covering, and a strange, colourless world stroked by silence emerges.

I was once told by a grizzled old farmer that the county of Yorkshire is bigger than Israel and covers more acres than words in the Bible. It may be something of an exaggeration, although Yorkshire folk are not prone to embellishing, but the county is certainly large.

facing page:
'The Yorkshire Dales' by Matthew Phinn.

In winter, when the crowds of 'off-comed-uns' have disappeared, the vastness and beauty of the great Dales fill me with a real sense of wonder.

During the ten years I was a school inspector in North Yorkshire, I came to know the children of the Dales very well, and became acquainted with their plain, honest, outspoken and disarming approach to life. I met many remarkable young people in the course of my work but there were some who stood out and made a deep impression upon me.

It was a chilly autumn day as I drove along to a small rural school in the depths of the Dales. The colouring of the scene was unforgettable: long belts of dark green firs glistening in an ocean of crimson heather, and grey woodsmoke rising to the pale purple of the sky. It was a cold, bright and silent world.

Andrew was eleven. He was poring over his book, his brow furrowed in concentration. As I approached he closed the book and placed a hand firmly on top.

"May I look at your work?" I asked, smiling.

"No," came the blunt reply.

"Why not?" I asked.

"Because it's not any good, that's why."

"I'd still like to see," I said.

"Well, tha can't." He kept a firm hand on his book so I could not verify his comments. "Can't read reight well, either," he added. "I have trouble wi' words." He looked up. "I'm remedial."

"Remedial," I repeated.

"Aye. I've got what's called 'special educational needs'. Not much good at owt."

"Everyone's good at something," I said.

He just shook his head in a resigned sort of way and stared out of the window to the distant hills.

"Where do you live?"

"Reight up theer." He pointed through the window to the far-off hills. "I live on a farm up theer — at t' top o' t' dale."

"What a lucky boy you are," I murmured. "You must have one of the finest views in the world."

"It's all reight," he said in a matter-of-fact voice. "What time were you up this mornin', then, mester?"

"Early," I replied. "Half past seven."

"Early? I was up at six helpin' me dad deliver a calf."

"Really?"

"And it were dead. It would've been a good milker an' all, wide solid rear and good udder texture. We got t' ratchet on..."

"Ratchet?" I interrupted.

"Aye, you put yer ratchet up against t' cow, it's a sort-of metal gadget, like. Yer tie yer ropes round t' calf's back legs and turn yer ratchet every time there's a contraction. Helping t' cow along." He paused. "Does tha know what a contraction is?"

"I do," I replied.

"Aye, it were dead all reight. So we've 'ad a month of it, I can tell thee," continued Andrew, fixing his eyes on a flock of sheep meandering between the grey limestone walls. He sighed. "Them sheep's ours," he then remarked casually. "We've got an 'undred yows and two jocks."

"Jocks?" I asked. "Are they Scottish sheep?"

He shook his dusty mop of hair. "No, no, jocks are rams, moor sheep. Does tha know why we has all them yows and only the two jocks?"

"Yes," I replied, smiling. "I think so."

"Bought another from t' market last week. It'd only been wi' us three days and it dropped down dead — even before it had done any tuppin'," he continued. "Me dad were none too pleased." He paused fractionally and gave a low whistle between his teeth. "Does tha know what tuppin' means?"

"Yes," I replied.

"We'd trouble week afore wi' t' 'oggits."

"Hoggits? Little pigs?" I ventured.

He shook his head again. "No, no, your 'oggits are sheep of an age between your lamb and your ewe. Sort of teenage sheep. Do you know what a shearling is, or a stot?"

I shook my head.

"A stirk or a teg?"

"I have no idea," I replied..

A slight smile came to the boy's lips and his expression took on that of the expert in the presence of an ignoramus — a sort of patient, sympathetic, tolerant look.

"Tha knows nowt abaat owt, theee, does tha?" he said.

"I'm remedial," I replied smiling.

Beneath a vast blue sky stretch the brilliant greens of Swaledale's pastureland dotted with lazy-looking sheep and criss-crossed with striding silvered limestone walls. Here is a land of beautiful valleys and vast empty moorland, soaring fells and eroded crags, dark scattered woodland and deep carved gorges, bubbling becks and tumbling waterfalls. Pictured above is the view up Swaledale across buttercup-filled meadows towards Gunnerside in the distance.

This stunning dale has not always been the idyllic farming country that it is today for it was once the centre of a thriving leadmining industry, centred around Gunnerside.

Swaledale, nestling in a deep winding valley, is one of the quietest and least spoilt of the Dales with a distinctive beauty all of its own.

Spectacular displays of colourful wild flowers are to be seen in the hay meadows (pictured above near Muker) in June and July. The meadows, which support a wide variety of wildlife as well as plants, are traditionally cleared of stock at the beginning of the growing season, usually during May, and receive only a light dressing of manure and an occasional liming. They are then cut for hay in the summer months, the hay used by farmers as winter feed for their stock.

Richmond was an important regional centre in the mediaeval period, when royal charters were granted giving rights to hold markets and fairs.

The Georgian era was one of great prosperity for the town when well-to-do visitors came to Richmond to attend the horse races, which took place at Richmond Racecourse. The King's Head Hotel, still present in the market place, was the main accommodation for the wealthy tourists. Grand houses were built at that time and surround the cobbled market place (pictured above), said to be one of the largest in England. The Church of the Holy Trinity rises from its centre.

Richmond, the name derived from the Norman French *riche-mont* meaning 'strong hill', is one of Yorkshire's most interesting towns.

The most impressive building is the imposing castle which occupies a defensive site on a steep hill above the fast-flowing River Swale. Founded by the Normans in 1071, the town grew up around this great stone castle, the massive keep of which dominates the town. In 1066, William I had given extensive lands to his followers as a reward for their support. Alan Rufus of Brittany, a kinsman of William, received the honour of Richmond and it was he who wasted no time in building the castle.

Pictured opposite is a view of the town and castle from Maison Dieu.

Bolton Castle is a magnificent mediaeval fortress, preserved in outstanding condition and situated in the heart of Wensleydale.

This thrusting pile of masonry with windows like sightless eyes must have appeared bleak and intimidating to a hapless Scottish queen. Mary, Queen of Scots, fled to England after losing the Battle of Langside in April 1568 and in July of that year was imprisoned at Bolton in the charge of Sir Henry, 9th Lord Scrope, who hurried north from Elizabeth's court to be her custodian. Mary appears to have been treated well, receiving many of the local Catholic nobility, many of whom were later involved in the Rising of the North. She remained at the castle until January 1569 when she was moved, in a fierce snowstorm, "further into the Realm, unto Tutburie".

Bolton Castle was defended for the king during the Civil War but fell on 5th November 1645 after a six-month siege, by which time the defenders had eaten the last horse in the castle. The garrison was allowed to depart with their colours flying. A Colonel Chaytor is reputed to have cut off his own hand and thrown it off the battlements at the besieging army in defiance.

Pages 82-3 following:
The view from the top of Malham Cove is regarded by the author Bill Bryson as "my favourite view on the earth". The broad, bare surface of the limestone pavement above Malham Cove, weather-scoured and crinkled, contrasts with the soft rounded hills beyond.

As we stared up at Malham Cove (pictured opposite), we A-Level students were asked by our geography master, Mr Taylor, if anyone knew the novel *The Water-babies* by Charles Kingsley. I had heard the story of Tom — the chimney sweep who meets the babies in the clear water — from my mother when I was younger. Mr Taylor related the story of how Charles Kingsley, having passed through Bradford and witnessed the squalor and filth there, visited Tarn House in Malham in 1858 as a guest of the millionaire philanthropist Walter Morrison. Kingsley was struck by the stark contrast of the dark industrial city and the stunning limestone scenery. He was a skilled botanist and was reputedly asked by the children of the house to explain the streaks of black on the face of the cove. He explained that they were made by a little chimney sweep called Tom slipping over the clifftop and sliding down into the stream. Here was his inspiration for the classic fantasy story.

Nearby Malham village (pictured above), surrounded by great domed hills, bone-white limestone cliffs and the broad acres of Malham Moor, is one of Yorkshire's most beautiful spots.

One of my favourite places in the Dales is the village of Arncliffe (pictured opposite) in Littondale.

Arncliffe Primary (pictured above) was the first school I visited when I became a school inspector in North Yorkshire (and also featured on the cover of my book *Gervase Phinn's Yorkshire*), and I can still recall the warmth of my welcome from the headteacher, Helen Clayton, the delightful children and the spectacular view from the classroom window. One Christmas when I visited the school, I was reminded of this delightful piece Ella Pontefract wrote in the first Christmas number of the *Dalesman* magazine in 1939:

"Perhaps our most vivid memory is of a visit just before Christmas to a nativity play, given in the soft dialect of Littondale. There was one small

angel, a chubby rosy-cheeked child with a beam of joy and goodwill on his face. We met him another day shouting in far from gentle language at an obstreperous cow, but the perfect cherub remains for us that tiny Dales boy, with a healthy face coloured by wind and weather."

At the centre of Wharfedale, which is one of the longest and most imposing of the limestone dales, is Grassington. Often described by locals as a village, it is really a small town, as indicated by its name and the fact that it was granted a charter for a market and fair in 1282, which continued to be held regularly until about 1860. Built around a cobbled market square (pictured above) — which is not, in fact, square at all — this quiet and unspoilt spot in the Dales has a variety of interesting buildings: the seventeenth-century Church House, the Black Horse Inn and the Devonshire Arms (pictured above to the left of the green water-pump). The eighteenth-century Grassington House (pictured right), with its tall sash windows, changed its use from a private house in the late 1870s and became a boarding house, thus heralding the birth of the tourist industry which is still so important to the town today.

The school at Grassington was a favourite of mine. I was always assured of a warm welcome, and was impressed by the high quality of the children's work and the dedication of the headteacher and staff.

I never left without hearing one of the many stories about the village, my favourite being the tale of the infamous Tom Lee. Tom Lee, who lived in the 1760s and was a miner and innkeeper of the Blue Anchor, was a notorious character. He harboured a grudge against the local doctor, Dr Petty, and murdered him. The doctor's body was eventually discovered, but the murderer was not identified until Lee's apprentice confessed some years later. Lee was tried at York, hanged, and his body gibbeted at what is now called Gibbet Hill in nearby Grass Wood (pictured above from the track to it from Grassington).

Leadmining near Grassington has been carried out since the fifteenth century. In 1750, the then Duke of Devonshire began a great development plan for the industry. He constructed a watercourse and erected a large new smelt mill together with a cupola, and the tall chimney that is still an important feature today (pictured above). The leadminers were a tough breed who enjoyed cockfighting, bear-baiting and heavy drinking, so it is no coincidence that Grassington police were the first to be armed in Britain.

Founded in 1674 by Matthew Hewitt, rector of Linton, to provide education in Latin 'with the necessary crafts of reading and writing', Threshfield School in Wharfedale (pictured above) is a particularly fine example of seventeenth-century Dales vernacular architecture. Readers of my Dales books will recognise Threshfield School which I loved to visit: "The small primary school was a lead-coloured stone building with porch, mullioned windows and an impressive solid door." Originally the building had one large schoolroom on the ground floor with two rooms for the schoolmaster above. Around 1875 the floor between the storeys was removed, giving the schoolroom a brighter and more spacious ambience.

Left, early morning in Threshfield.

Ilkley Moor is the site of the famous Cow and Calf, a large millstone grit rock formation consisting of an outcrop and boulder, also known as Hangingstone Rocks. They are so named because one is large, with the smaller one sitting close to it, like a cow and her calf.

According to local legend, the Calf was split from the Cow when the giant Rombald was fleeing an enemy and stamped on the rock as he leapt across the valley. The enemy, it is said, was his angry wife. She dropped the stones held in her skirt to form the local rock formation, the Skirtful of Stones.

It was here at the nearby Cow and Calf Inn that I met my future father-in-law and mother-in-law when my girlfriend's parents invited me for lunch (to give me the once-over).

Ilkley, with its fine residences and villas, cafés and tea rooms, tree-lined avenues, varied shops and pleasant gardens, and the famous Ilkley Moor nearby, was a favourite venue for my future wife Christine and I to visit when we were courting. It was in Bettys Tea Rooms in Ilkley (pictured left), as I stared at Christine across the tiered tray of finger sandwiches and cakes, that I decided to ask her to marry me.

Ilkley Moor (facing page left) is the highest part of Rombalds Moor, the bleak stretch of moorland between Ilkley and Keighley, and the inspiration for Yorkshire's anthem *On Ilkla Mooar Baht 'At*. Legend has it that there is a phantom hound which roams the moor after sunset and if seen foretells of death or a great tragedy.

West Yorkshire

facing page:
'Sandal Castle' by Matthew Phinn.

My initial impression of Leeds, on my first visit to the city as a child of seven, was not a very favourable one.

It was a cold, dark and drizzly Saturday afternoon when I caught a train from Rotherham Masborough Station with my mother. My face had been scrubbed red, hair plastered down, shoes polished and I was attired in my smartest outfit. My mother was on a mission. She was a devout Roman Catholic but she fell out with the parish priest, Father Hammond, over my education. As a school nurse she had a very good overview of the teaching and learning which took place in Rotherham's schools. She was fiercely ambitious that I should succeed and decided to send me to a state primary school rather than the Roman Catholic one. Father Hammond was not best pleased and told my mother in no uncertain terms that she had a clear duty to provide me with a Catholic education. He then told her that if she did not follow his directive he would refuse her communion. It hurt her deeply and she felt the injustice but she did not change her mind about my schooling.

That memorable Saturday I went to Leeds with her to petition the bishop. Bishop Heenan listened quietly at my mother's *cri de coeur* but he refused to intervene on her behalf and we left his office next to St Anne's Roman Catholic Cathedral despondent. We caught a train straight home.

My second visit to Leeds was three years later and under very different circumstances. One afternoon, just before Christmas, my father took me to see the pantomime at the

City Varieties. We walked through the city crowded with shoppers. It was one of the few very special occasions when it was just me and my Dad, no brothers or sister. Everywhere was bustling and colourful. There were the Christmas lights, the amazing shops, a brass band playing in the streets, vendors selling hot potatoes and chestnuts and the atmosphere of Christmas.

The City Varieties is the oldest extant music hall in the country, an intimate, colourful and atmospheric little theatre, hidden between two arcades. I fell in love with it. All the greats of variety theatre have performed there: Charlie Chaplin and Houdini, Tommy Cooper and Hylda Baker, Marie Lloyd and Les Dawson and, of course, the legendary Ken Dodd who takes some persuading to leave the stage once he's started.

I appeared there myself in 2006 in my one-man-show. Before my performance I stood on the empty stage looking down at the empty stalls and recalled a small boy sitting on a plush red velvet seat with his father, his eyes (as we say in Yorkshire) 'like chapel hat pegs', entering a magical world of the pantomime.

In October 1966 Uncle Ted in his white van took me, my case and books, electric kettle, toaster and my portable Olivetti typewriter to Leeds where I spent the next four years studying for my degree and certificate in education. Apart from the school trips to the Isle of Man, the annual fortnight in Blackpool and the brief encounter with camping in Derbyshire, I had never been away from home.

My enthusiasm and eagerness the evening before setting off to train as a teacher was palpable. The great wide world awaited me, a world of new friends and greater challenges and I embraced it with open arms. It was the start of an exciting adventure and where better to begin than in this bright, thriving, vibrant city. I soon came to love Leeds — the theatres, shops, restaurants, museums and the friendliness of the people.

As part of my teacher-training I was sent on teaching practice to Huddersfield, Wakefield and Menston, and came to know parts of West Yorkshire well. A long teaching practice in a Wakefield secondary school meant I saw much of the city and its environs, the atmospheric ruins of Sandal Castle being my favourite spot.

I returned to Wakefield some years later to present the prizes and certificates at Wakefield High School for Girls. One young woman gained a remarkable five top grades at A-Level. I congratulated her and asked to which university she was going. She was an articulate young woman, and our conversation continued. Mrs Langham, the formidable headmistress, indicated discreetly with a small nod of her head that I should move on. Mischievously, I continued chatting to the student, much to the amusement of the audience. Later the chairman of governors remarked, tongue in cheek, that it was the first time in the history of the school that a speaker had ignored the headmistress on her own stage.

Fifty years ago cities and towns like Leeds and Bradford were full of dust and soot as the great machines of industry polluted the air and turned town halls into immense grim monuments and houses to blackened rows. The pioneering Titus Salt left the dirt and grime of industrial Bradford in the 1850s to set up a huge T-shaped mill, Italianate in style, near Shipley and founded a whole new community called Saltaire where the air was cleaner and the environment much healthier.

By the 1960s when I arrived in Leeds to study, the decline in woollen and worsted manufacturing had continued, and some of the mills had been adapted for light industry and commercial use. Many of the buildings had been restored and cleaned, and revealed themselves to be impressive and individual and not without architectural merit.

In 1974 I met my future wife, Christine, a 'Yorkshire lass', born and bred in Shipley, and educated at Bingley Grammar School. Now a new part of Yorkshire was revealed to me: Shipley Glen, Saltaire, Five Rise Locks, Haworth, Bradford and, of course, Ilkley (featured in the previous chapter).

Christine's father, the legendary 'Legs' Bentley, who captained Yorkshire at rugby and was president of Yorkshire RUFC, was at great pains to point out to me when I first met him that West Yorkshire has all the stunning landscapes and history of the northern, southern and eastern parts of the county: windswept uplands and verdant lowlands, reservoirs and rivers, castles and stately homes. Who was I to argue with my future father-in-law?

Pages 98-9 following, Salts Mill, built by the industrial philanthropist Sir Titus Salt and which forms the centrepiece of the model village of Saltaire.

The story of Titus Salt, the self-made man who became one of Yorkshire's best known, most successful and admired sons, is a fascinating one.

Born near Leeds in 1803, the eldest of six children, he joined his father's small business at eighteen as a wool-stapler. When he was about twenty-eight, he bought some Donskoi wool from Russia, but because it was difficult to process the tangled fibres, he could not sell it. He decided to buy a mill of his own and began to spin the wool himself. He prospered and could soon afford to buy four more mills in Bradford town centre.

Having made a fortune in alpaca and mohair, he decided to move his business away from the overcrowded and polluted town of Bradford, and into the country. The new green-field site was a few miles away near Shipley, adjoining the Leeds-Liverpool Canal, the River Aire and the newly made railway station. The vast T-shaped mill, constructed in Italianate style, opened in 1853 on Titus Salt's fiftieth birthday.

After becoming virtually derelict in the 1980s, Salts Mill was given a new lease of life thanks to the imaginative and dedicated efforts of the late Jonathan Silver who transformed the site into one of Yorkshire's treasures. Salts Mill today is home to the prestigious 1853 Gallery which houses a permanent exhibition of the works of the world-renowned and Bradford born artist David Hockney. The Hockney galleries are only part, however, of this amazing complex. There is a huge shop (pictured above) selling books, prints and posters, retail outlets which offer everything from early musical instruments to designer jewellery, and an excellent restaurant.

Titus Salt was an enlightened and philanthropic employer. He envisaged a community centred on the massive mill, with workers given high-quality housing and opportunities for education, recreation and healthcare. An entire village of houses, park, school, library, recreation and learning institute, and outdoor sports facilities was created, along with the splendid United Reformed church.

The church was built in 1859 by the town's architects Henry Lockwood and William Mawson in a classically Italianate style, with a portico supported by Corinthian columns surmounted by a tower and cupola. Inside (pictured left) is a sumptuous interior in cream, pink and pale blue, with scagiola columns and a pair of huge chandeliers. In the church porch is a memorial bust of Sir Titus Salt, carved by Thomas Milnes. Milnes was born in Yorkshire, and his other sculptural works include the four lions at each corner of nearby Victoria Square.

Over a span of twenty years, Titus Salt's model village of Saltaire saw the construction of 820 long solid terraced houses, built in Yorkshire stone to accommodate the 4,500 mill workers. The streets were named after his eleven children and family. In 1876 the last building in Saltaire was completed.

In December of that same year Sir Titus Salt died at his home. The city of Bradford honoured him with a civic funeral, attended by 100,000 people, and he was buried in the family mausoleum in the United Reformed church in Saltaire.

River navigation was unable to solve all Yorkshire's transport problems during the Industrial Revolution, so canals were cut into the landscape. With the Pennines being so hilly, locks had to be introduced to raise or lower the level of the Leeds-Liverpool Canal.

This stretch of the canal at Bingley is home to a masterpiece of civil engineering: the Five Rise Locks. It was described at the time of its opening in the *Leeds Intelligencer* as "the noblest works of the kind". Designed by John Longbotham of Halifax and constructed in ashlar millstone grit by local stonemasons, it comprises the steepest flight of locks in Britain, with a gradient of about one in five. The Leeds-Liverpool Canal ascends by this extraordinary staircase high above the town: over a distance of 320 feet (100 m), boats are raised nearly 60 feet (18 m). In March 1774 at the official opening, 30,000 people turned out to celebrate to the sound of guns, cheering and music.

The gaunt remains of Kirkstall Abbey near Leeds are still impressively majestic and evocative. Completed between 1152 and 1182 in Bramley Fall gritstone, the abbey still stands substantially to its full height and represents one of the most complete examples of a mediaeval Cistercian abbey in Britain. It was within these ruined walls that I did much of my courting when a student in Leeds.

Leeds was one of only six 'civic universities' which were granted royal charters at the beginning of the twentieth century. I spent many an hour working and revising within the walls of the Brotherton Building, which is at the heart of the university. The distinctive tower of the Parkinson Building (pictured above) forms the university logo. Three of the Phinn family are graduates of this world-renowned teaching institute.

Leeds City Varieties is a Grade II listed building and a rare surviving example of the Victorian music halls of the 1850s and 1860s. Built in 1865 by local pub landlord Charles Thornton, the theatre was an extension to the music room of the White Swan Inn and was originally called Thornton's New Music Hall & Fashionable Lounge. The name subsequently changed to the White Swan Varieties, then Stansfield's Varieties and the City Palace of Varieties. Despite changes of name and ownership, the theatre has remained virtually the same since the late nineteenth century. Behind the unprepossessing façade there is a gem of an interior, a long rectangle with boxes separated by cast-iron columns along the sides at circle level.

Designed by Vincent Harris in 1926, the imposing Leeds Civic Hall (pictured above) was officially opened on 23rd August 1933 by King George V. Its two giant gilded owls — symbols of the City of Leeds — overlook Millennium Square and the equally imposing town hall (pictured left). The building, which cost £360,000 to construct, accommodates the lord mayor, city treasurer and city council. It was in one of the lavish great halls of Leeds Civic Hall that I received an honorary fellowship from Leeds Trinity University College in 2010.

Sited on a commanding ridge overlooking the River Calder, near the town of Wakefield, are the remains of the once-great Sandal Castle.

Founded by William de Warenne in the twelfth century as an earthwork motte-and-bailey fortress, it was strengthened during the thirteenth century to become a formidable stone stronghold.

When training as a teacher, I spent my teaching practice at St Thomas à Becket Roman Catholic High School, a stone's throw from the castle. Some lunchtimes I would walk the short distance and have my sandwiches sitting amidst the ruins. It is now a tranquil and atmospheric spot, but what a violent history it has had.

These jagged walls of stone have a strong resonance for Yorkshire folk, for it was here that one of the bloodiest and most decisive battles of the Wars of the Roses took place. In 1460, Richard Plantagenet, Duke of York, made a bid for the throne. Initially he received little support but he pressed his claim, and an Act of Accord was made in October 1460 recognising him as heir to the throne and naming him Protector of the Realm. In December, Richard went to Sandal Castle with an army of 3,000 to 8,000 men to meet his Lancastrian enemies. He was soundly beaten at the Battle of Wakefield, captured, beheaded and his head displayed on Micklegate Bar in York.

Two centuries later, Sandal Castle was one of the "ruins that Cromwell knocked about a bit". Although in 1642, at the start of the Civil War, Sandal Castle was in a state of disrepair, local Royalists under the command of Major Ward were determined to hold it for the king and defended it resolutely. During his time in command the only event of note to happen was that the unfortunate commander tripped down some stairs in the castle, broke his neck and died. When it finally fell into the hands of the Parliamentarian forces on the 1st October 1645, the garrison of ten officers and ninety men received a safe passage to Welbeck House in Nottinghamshire. The following year Parliament demolished enough of the castle to ensure that it could never be used again.

Chantry chapels were so called because each chapel was served by its own priest or priests whose duty was to say masses or chant dirges for the souls of the dead. Before the Reformation such chapels were occasionally built on bridges for travellers to give thanks for their safe arrival in a town after a journey.

Today, there are only four such chapels remaining in England. Yorkshire is fortunate enough to have two of the surviving bridge chapels: one at Rotherham (see page 135), the other at Wakefield.

The latter, the Chantry Chapel of St Mary the Virgin, is the oldest and most elaborate. Situated just south of the city of Wakefield on the nine-arch bridge over the River Calder, the chapel's history dates back over 650 years. After the Dissolution of the Monasteries, the former chapel, like the one at Rotherham, was put to a variety of secular uses, including that of a warehouse, library, corn factor's office and even a cheesecake shop.

In 1842 the newly formed Yorkshire Architectural Society, keen to restore this prized mediaeval building to its former glory, appointed the architect George Gilbert Scott to undertake the renovation. Rather than repair the worn and decayed centuries-old west front, Scott completely replaced the original richly carved mediaeval façade which was taken to Kettlethorpe Hall. Here it became the frontage to a folly boathouse on an artificial lake. It was later destroyed by vandals.

Walton Hall, near Wakefield, was the home of Charles Waterton, naturalist, taxidermist and eccentric who, in the early nineteenth century, travelled the world collecting rare species and, on his return, created the world's first nature reserve in West Yorkshire.

Waterton inspired Charles Darwin and many other scientists, and was England's first eco-campaigner, an outspoken, pioneering conservationist, a passionate man who despised the destruction of the natural environment, especially when wilfully done.

After his travels, Waterton enclosed 250 acres (100 ha) at his home with an eight-foot (2.5 m) high wall which ran for three miles (5 km). He opened his estate to the public so people could enjoy the wildfowl sanctuary he had created.

Today Walton Hall is a hotel, conference and leisure centre, and the park is a golf course although there are several public footpaths.

In 1988 the National Coal Mining Museum for England opened at Caphouse Colliery, situated on the western edge of the Yorkshire coalfield. Coal had been mined here for centuries and today Caphouse reputedly has the oldest existing coal-mine shaft still in everyday use in Britain today. By 1985 the coal at Caphouse was exhausted and its conversion to a museum began.

Visitors are given a fascinating insight into the life of the coal miner. They descend 450 feet (140 m) underground and are taken on a tour of the workings by a guide, an ex-miner, who shares his mining experiences.

Much of the original colliery buildings (some of which are over 130 years old) still survive, including the original pithead, the 1876 steam winder, the pithead baths and the medical centre. The Coal Interface Gallery demonstrates how machinery was used to hew the coal.

South Yorkshire

Bradford for cash,
Halifax for dash,
Wakefield for pride and for poverty.
Huddersfield for show,
Sheffield what's low,
Leeds for dirt and vulgarity.
Barnsley for ale,
Doncaster for rail,
And Rotherham for great singularity.

(*English Folklore* by A R Wright, 1928)

facing page:
'Roche Abbey' by Matthew Phinn.

I knew from an early age that there was something rather different about the town in which I was born. I was vaguely aware that there was something distinct about Rotherham.

In the popular mind it was (and I guess still is) the butt of the comedian's joke ("Rotherham doesn't have a twin town, it has a suicide pact with Grimsby", "The town's like a cemetery with lights"). Rotherham is viewed in the popular mind as a dark, depressing, brooding Northern industrial place with little to commend it. The image was one where steelworks belch out acrid smoke, pit heads ruin the landscape, men in flat caps and mufflers, cigarettes dangling from their mouths, drag whippets behind them, grubby urchins play on narrow cobbled streets, muscular women donkey-stone the steps of their terraced houses and running through the centre is the pungent-smelling polluted river the colour of khaki. It's grim up North.

Well it was certainly not "grim up North" when I was growing up. In walking distance were two public baths, two parks, several cinemas, a theatre, the towering Norman church of All Saints, and all the shops in a vibrant and bustling town centre. A bus ride away was Sheffield where I went in search of coins and stamps, to cheer on United and sometimes take a camping trip by train into Derbyshire. In cycling distance were the ruins of the once-spectacular fortress of Conisbrough, the remains of the great Roche Abbey set in a wooded ravine, small villages to explore and acres of open countryside.

After reading Walker Scott's epic romance of the brave knight Ivanhoe and the beautiful Lady Rowena, I cycled out one bright Saturday morning to Conisbrough Castle. The castle, which rises majestically from a mound overlooking the River Don, was a deserted roofless shell when I was a boy but it had retained its grandeur. I recall sitting beneath the perimeter wall staring up at the imposing edifice and imagining knights in glittering armour, gallant Crusaders, dastardly villains, jousting and sieges, dark dungeons and great battles. Scott, who must have visited the castle and been impressed by it, made it the setting for his novel *Ivanhoe*. The picture he paints of events and people at Conisbrough, in the reign of Richard the Lionheart, I discovered some years later (and much to my disappointment) is entirely fictitious. By then, the keep would only just have been built and there were no enclosing stone walls. It's still a cracking story, though.

In 1956, I came upon Wentworth Woodhouse. Our class of forty-plus pupils was bussed out one bright sunny Monday morning from Broom Valley Juniors to Wentworth, a village twixt Rotherham and Barnsley, so that the female students training there to be PE mistresses could "practise on us".

The redoubtable Lady Mabel Smith, sister of the sixth Earl Fitzwilliam, with the keen social conscience of the more liberally minded aristocrat, suggested turning Wentworth into a school and in 1947 she used her not inconsiderable eloquence and influence to get the West Riding County Council to take on the house on a fifty-year lease.

This historic mansion subsequently became a training college for female PE teachers and named the Lady Mabel

Wentworth village, between Barnsley and Rotherham. The village dates back to 1066 and is linked with three local families, the Wentworths, the Watsons and the Fitzwilliams. It was to Wentworth that I and my school pals journeyed in the mid-1950s to be "practised upon" by the rather lovely female student PE teachers of Lady Mabel College (formerly the imposing mansion of Wentworth Woodhouse).

College in her honour. In 1979, when the maintenance costs proved too prohibitive, the college closed and nine years later Lady Elizabeth Hastings, the tenth earl's granddaughter and beneficiary, put the house up for sale. Today the vast building stands in its lonely acres, stark and shuttered, the home of a recluse, its great iron gates closed to the public.

So, as an impressionable ten year old, I got my first sighting of Wentworth Woodhouse. I had read about such buildings in the history books but never seen such an immense edifice. I recall climbing down from the bus in my PE kit of white vest, black shorts and plimsolls (which we called pumps) to see what looked like a huge cardboard cutout. It was breathtaking. I marvelled at the great stone pillars, ornate pediments, porticos and domed pavilions (although I had no idea what these were called at the time), and the many hundreds of windows. Of course, we small urchins were not allowed to ascend the flight of steep stone steps and enter into this palace. We were lined up on the lawns to the front of the house ready to be "practised upon".

It was not an altogether unpleasant experience for me and my pals to be "practised upon" by tall, willowy young women in short skirts and tight-fitting blouses, with soft smiles and long legs, and who helped us with our physical exertions: star jumps and squat thrusts, hand springs and forward rolls, handstands and press-ups. After half an hour of stretching and

Pages 114-5 following: Roche Abbey, a view of the transept walls from the monks' choir.

jumping, leaping and running we were allowed to rest. That morning I lay on my stomach staring across the parkland dotted with grazing deer, avenues of tall cedars, manicured lawns, borders bursting with colourful flowers, pale statues and spouting fountains. I had never seen anything like it.

I heard a great deal about Steel, Peech and Tozer, the great steelworks where my father spent his whole working life, but I had never been inside. This huge works, in which teeming molten steel was poured from one-hundred-ton cradles into ingot moulds and later rolled into billets and bars, was where he started work when he came out of the army. He then moved into the 'finishing shop' where his job was to chip out faults (scarfing) in the metal as the steel billets rolled out in the finishing bank. Years later, when I visited the magnificent Magna, the industrial museum now sited in the Don Valley, it was only then that I fully realised what an unpleasant and dangerous job my father had, and what a very special man he must have been to have endured that smoky smouldering hell day after day, night after night, and never complain.

One day, when I was in the fourth year at school, Mr Williams, the headmaster, stopped me in the corridor. He looked at me with striking earnestness before asking: "Do you go to the theatre, young Phinn?"

"I've been to the Regent in Rotherham, sir," I told him. "To see the pantomime and some of the variety shows."

"Pah! Pantomime, variety shows," he repeated dismissively. "Have you seen plays — proper plays? Shakespeare? Ben Jonson? Marlowe? Ibsen?"

"No sir," I replied.

He drew in a slow breath. "You ought to go to the theatre. Never mind the television and the cinema; it's the theatre — the window onto the world."

"Yes sir," I said as he disappeared down the corridor, his black gown fluttering behind him.

I thought no more about it but the following week Mr Williams stopped me again after assembly.

"Two tickets here," he said, thrusting an envelope into my hand, "for the Sheffield Lyceum. You'll enjoy it."

Spruced up and with a rather reluctant friend in tow, I took the bus to Sheffield the following Saturday night to see a production of Sheridan's classic comedy *The Rivals*. I had been in a theatre before when I had been taken to the pantomimes as a small child and to the end of the pier shows at Blackpool, but I had never been in a theatre as grand as the Lyceum. I was overwhelmed by the gaudy splendour of the great building with the ornate painted plaster ceiling, red velvet covered seats, the great crimson curtains and the highly decorated arch above the stage. The floodlit stage, the sparkle and glitter, the chattering audience which surrounded me, the actors in their colourful costumes, intoxicated me. I entered a different world.

It was that small encounter with and the intervention of Mr Williams that started my love affair with the theatre, and soon I was a regular theatre-goer. I would catch the bus to Sheffield to see the touring companies at the Playhouse and the Lyceum, or watch the Rotherham Rep at the Civic Theatre. I saw classic dramas and farces, musicals and period pieces and would often see Mr Williams in the expensive seats nodding at me approvingly.

Alec, my brother, loved animals. He had the usual pets youngsters like to keep — rabbits, tortoises, hamsters, mice and budgerigars — but he kept a ferret in a small hutch and a grass snake in a glass tank. Then he became fascinated with birds of prey. He found a young kestrel which, like the fictional Billy Casper in Barry Hine's classic novel *A Kestrel for a Knave*, he trained to hunt. Alec would take the kestrel, which gripped onto the large leather gauntlet which he wore, up Moorgate Road to Boston Park where he would let the bird fly free. It wheeled and fluttered in the air until my brother swung the coloured lure (a bunch of feathers with a lump of meat attached to a long string) above his head and the bird would return to his gloved fist. It was thrilling to watch. Once the kestrel, high in an empty sky, hovered and then plummeted downwards. The next minute a small bird fell tumbling to the ground in a flurry of beating wings. The kestrel sheared away and then dropped to the ground onto its prey. It wasn't long before the bird, having had the taste of freedom, took off and never returned. Alec spent hours in Boston Park looking for it … but to no avail.

Until Brodsworth Hall was reopened by English Heritage in 1995 following a major programme of restoration and conservation, few had seen this hidden gem in Yorkshire's industrial heartland. Situated five miles (8 km) north-west of Doncaster, Brodsworth is one of the most complete surviving examples of a Victorian country house and has remained virtually unchanged since the 1860s. When Charles Sabine Augustus Thellusson inherited the estate in 1859, he commissioned the renowned architect Chevalier Casentini, whom he had met in Italy, to build him a suitably grand residence in the Italianate style. The result is an impressively solid, formal building.

The fifteen acres (6 ha) of gardens, really a series of 'grand gardens in miniature', have been restored authentically to show what the Victorian gentry would have enjoyed at Brodsworth in its heyday. Features like the formal garden with the unusual three-tired Italian marble dolphin centrepiece, summerhouse, fern dell, pet cemetery and topiary, are fine examples of Victorian 'gardening book design'. Of special interest are the restored woodland garden and the magnificent display of blooms in the rose dell. A new garden, incorporating both formal and informal features, was created amidst the surrounding landscaped parkland.

There are over thirty rooms in Brodsworth Hall, ranging from the grand reception rooms such as the drawing room (pictured above) with their original furnishings and fixtures, to the servants' quarters.

Rich decoration, Corinthian columns, hand-painted wallpaper, chandeliers and gilded mirrors, sculptures and oil paintings, all reflect the once-great wealth of the Thellusson family.

A succession of white marble statues runs from the entrance hall to the pillared south hall (pictured right) and, of all the sculptures, Argenti's *Sleeping Venus* is particularly striking.

The real fascination about this remarkable house is that it has been preserved with all the wear-and-tear of family life over more than a century, for English Heritage, which manages Brodsworth, made the imaginative decision to conserve the interior 'as found' rather than restoring it.

A favourite day out for the Phinn family, when the children were small, was Cusworth Hall, Museum & Park (pictured opposite and above).

Situated to the west of Doncaster and one of only four listed Grade I buildings in the district, Cusworth was first mentioned as 'Cuzeuuorde' in the Domesday survey of 1086, but there had been a settlement here for centuries dating back to the Anglo-Saxon period.

In the eighteenth century William Wrightson commissioned George Platt, a local builder and architect, to design and build a house in keeping with his status and position. Wrightson was married twice; both wives brought with them considerable wealth which enabled him to make extensive additions to this fine Georgian house. It was refaced and extended by James Paine between 1749 and 1753.

The Wrightson family had considerable influence in the area, and family members were involved in local and national politics, both making and administering the law as MPs and JPs. They controlled appointments to the church, schools and even admissions to hospitals and workhouses. By the nineteenth century the Cusworth estate consisted of a vast 20,000 acres (8,100 ha), the Wrightsons owning farms, houses and lands in surrounding villages and towns including Tickhill, Adwick-le-Street and Conisbrough.

Like many a large estate, after the First World War, Cusworth declined. The house and park were sold to the Doncaster Council in 1961, and became a museum and public park.

The towering Norman fortress of Conisbrough Castle (pictured above and opposite), built by the fifth Earl Warenne in the late 1180s, rises majestically from a mound overlooking the River Don. The spectacular cylindrical keep, with its mighty ninety-foot (27 m) tower and six mighty buttresses, was constructed from white ashlar stone and was considered to be impregnable. Following the death of its owners, the Warenne family, Conisbrough Castle rapidly lost its importance and by the end of the 1400s it had been abandoned as a residence. Ironically, it was its state of disrepair that saved it from destruction during the Civil War.

For me it is the most impressive mediaeval building in South Yorkshire.

Pictured above are participants in one of the regular mediaeval re-enactment days staged at the castle.

The monks of Roche picked a perfect location for their abbey at Maltby Beck, near Rotherham. In 1147 they began building this impressively beautiful structure in a verdant, peaceful, rock-bound valley with clear streams. Roche Abbey stood for 400 years until the Dissolution of the Monasteries, during the reign of Henry VIII, when, like other monastic houses, it was suppressed, the monks dispersed and the abbey buildings destroyed and pillaged for the stone. Little remains of the once-proud abbey, but one can sense by the outlines of the stones how huge and imposing this building must have been.

I recently returned on a cold winter's morning, when there was a light dusting of snow on the ancient stone and a watery sunshine struggled to make its way through the heavy December sky. There was no sound or movement, and I was at once again aware of the spirituality and tranquillity of this awesome place. Some things we see in life are soon forgotten, others never leave us. The memory of my first view of Roche Abbey has stayed with me, like an oil painting … an enduring masterpiece.

When I was eleven I remember climbing up the internal staircase of Keppel's Column (a few miles south of Wentworth Woodhouse) to the very top and viewing the miles of surrounding countryside. Sadly, the tower is now in a dangerous condition and is kept locked.

This unusual monument is 115 feet (35 m) in height but was originally planned to be even taller and capped with a statue of Admiral Keppel, but evidently the Marquess of Rockingham, who funded the project, ran short of money. The tower was designed by John Carr, who was also responsible for the Wentworth Woodhouse stables and the family's Irish house at Collattin. Admiral Keppel was a friend of the marquess and a fellow Whig who was court-martialled following a naval defeat at the hands of the French in 1777. The marquess had already planned to build a pillar to mark the southern boundary of his parkland but, following Keppel's acquittal, he adapted the design to create a triumphal pillar to celebrate what he saw as a defeat for the government.

Wentworth House was once the palatial residence of the earls Fitzwilliam. Built in the 1720s for Thomas Wentworth, later Marquess of Rockingham, this vast, imposing stately home, with its six-hundred-foot (180 m) long Palladian east front — the longest country-house façade in Europe — five miles (8 km) of passageways and a room for every day of the year, took over sixteen years to complete. The surrounding park had upwards of 1,500 acres (600 ha) of vast lawns and majestic woods, ornamented by temples, columns and picturesque water features. After a colourful catalogue of family indiscretions, endless arguments, forbidden loves, contentious court cases, feuds and financial setbacks, the residence became a white elephant, too big and expensive to manage.

As a boy, I remember well the bumpy bus ride from Rotherham to Sheffield via Attercliffe, past 'Steelos' — the nickname for the Templeborough steelworks of Steel, Peech and Tozer (now Magna Science Adventure Centre), where my father worked for thirty or more years. Down the depressing Don Valley rattled the blue and white double-decker bus, past dirty corrugated iron sheds, yards of scrap, rusty cranes and huge overhead transporters. It was an area that contained little but dust, dirt and an incredible ugliness. Until the 1960s, steelmaking was a hard and dangerous process, a world of noise, heat, oil, dust and dirt. Hundreds of men worked day and night stoking row upon row of smoke-belching, coal-fired, open-hearth furnaces. I really do not know how my father stood it for so long.

Magna is based within the former Templeborough steelworks in Rotherham. A £46 million Millennium Lottery grant has enabled the building to be transformed into one of the country's most spectacular 'working' museums with futuristic technology, striking displays (such as the Fire Tornado, pictured left; and the Big Melt, pictured on pages 130-1), visionary architecture, and imaginative interactive games and challenges. The original features, including hulking hooks and cranes and winding passages, have been left untouched, to give visitors a feel for what this great steelworks once produced: over one and a quarter million tonnes of cast ingots a year, and much of the steel needed in both world wars.

FIRE

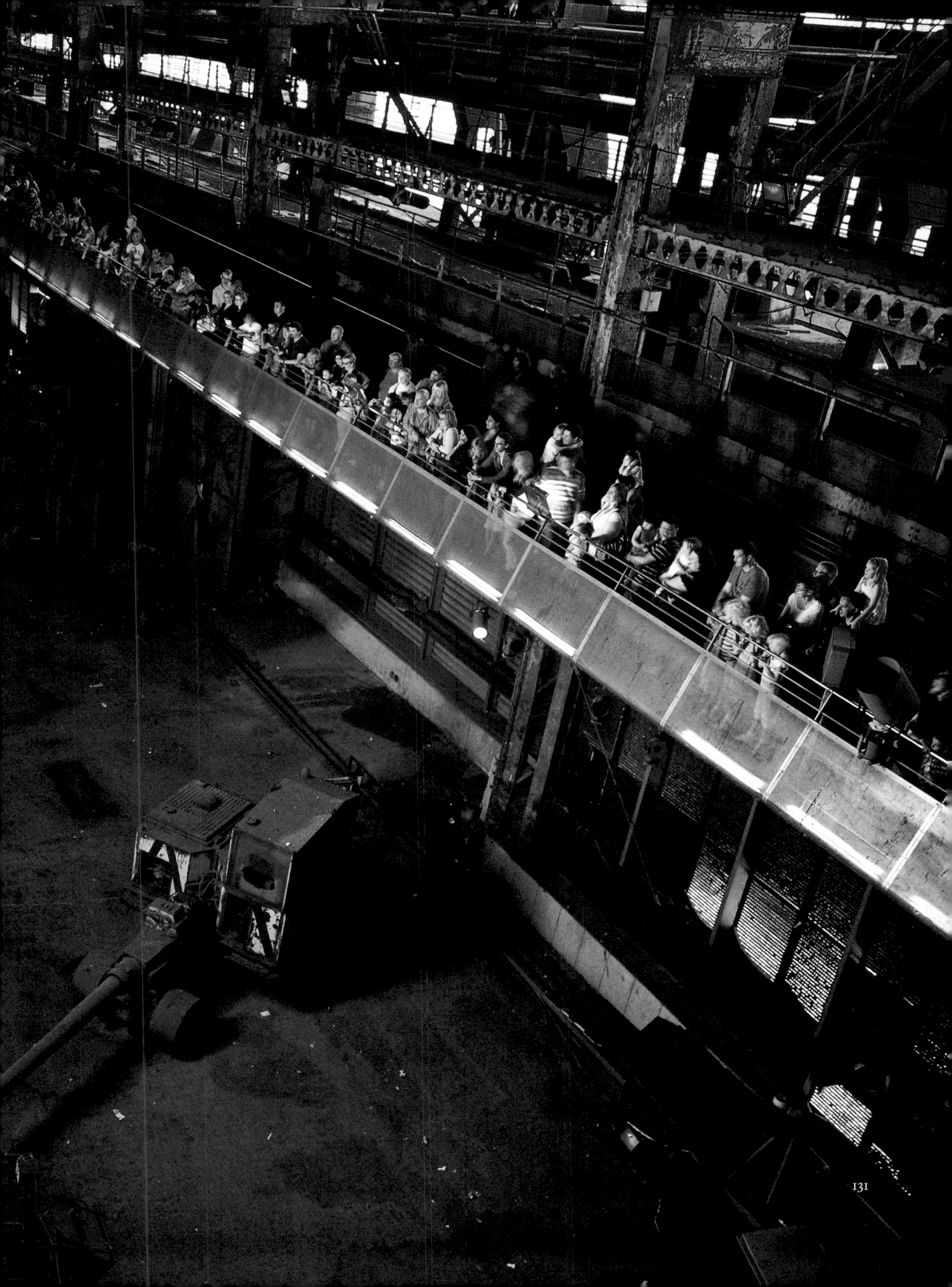

As a child a favourite haunt of mine was Boston Park, Rotherham's first public park, which opened its gates in 1876. At the entrance stood a small, squat building known as 'Boston Castle', with battlements and square mullioned windows, erected as a hunting lodge by the Earl of Effingham who originally owned the land. The local newspaper, the *Rotherham Advertizer*, once described the folly as 'a castellated pigeon cote'. Completed in 1775, Boston Castle was probably named after the Boston Tea Party by the earl. He was something of a maverick and supported the American cause in the War of Independence. When he leased the area to Rotherham Corporation for conversion to a park, he insisted that the opening ceremony took place on the 4th July, the centenary of the Declaration of Independence.

The old photograph (below right) of Boston Castle dates from around 1910-12. The sculptures set in the wall (right) relate to the Rotherham & Sheffield Railway opened in 1838. Neither of these pieces is there now. The crest probably came from the Rotherham terminus station on Westgate (this is now in Rotherham Archives). The bust was of John Stephenson (no relation to George). He was involved in the financing and laying out of the railway. Nobody knows where the bust is today. The structure to the left of the castle had a drinking fountain in it — this too has gone now to make way for space for cars to park. All of these sculptures hark back to a time when Boston Park was seen as a resting place for all sorts of 'unattached' sculptural architecture from the town — all of which has now gone.

I spent many a happy hour as a child and as a teenager at Clifton Park (pictured top left). In those days the park had a children's paddling pool, cenotaph, bandstand with sliding glass doors, Roman remains re-sited from Templeborough, memorial gardens, rock gardens, lawns and picnic areas and, my favourite, the museum.

The most interesting exhibit in the museum was not the amazing Rhinoceros Vase, the first ever porcelain vase cast in one piece, but Nelson, the huge, snarling stuffed lion in the glass case. Even in the 1950s the old 'King of Beasts' looked worse for wear.

Sometimes on warm summer Sunday evenings my parents would take me to the park to sit around the domed and pillared bandstand (pictured bottom left) to listen to the Salvation Army or one of the colliery bands.

The Municipal Borough of Rotherham (now Rotherham Council) purchased Clifton House and grounds in 1891 for £25,000. The house was built in 1783 and previously owned by the Walker family who were early industrialists involved in the manufacture of iron and steel. Clifton Park was opened to the public on 25th June 1891.

The opening ceremony, performed by Edward, Prince of Wales, was, by all accounts, a memorable affair, attended by thousands who were entertained with fireworks and bands. The high point of the festivities was perhaps not the ascent by Captain Whelan in a hot-air balloon but when one of the town councillors became entangled in the ropes and was unceremoniously lifted off the ground by his legs as the balloon rose. Fortunately, the poor man managed to disentangle himself.

The Lyceum Theatre was opened in 1897 and is the last example of an Edwardian auditorium in Sheffield. With seating in the magnificently refurbished auditorium for over a thousand, this listed building was designed by W G R Sprague as a traditional proscenium arch theatre.

As a child I loved (and still do) the pantomimes with their simple plots where good always triumphed, the outrageous cross-dressing characters, the doggerel, the ridiculously silly jokes and play on words, the foolish antics, the bright colours, the gaudy costumes, the lively music and the audience participation where you were encouraged to shout out as loud as you could. For many years the Lyceum, during the months between Christmas Eve and Easter, staged a panto, with visiting producers bringing famous actors and variety turns to entertain local families twice a day. In the 1940s the Lyceum began to produce its own pantomime, and stars of radio such as Morecambe and Wise, Harry Secombe and Frankie Howerd appeared in stage here.

Following its closure in 1968, the Lyceum took on different uses including a bingo hall and a rock venue before undergoing a £12 million renovation and reopening in 1991.

The town centre of Rotherham is dominated by the great red sandstone church of All Saints with its impressive 180-foot (55m) spire. Built in the thirteenth century, it is described by Pevsner as "the best perpendicular church in the country", and by Simon Jenkins in his book *England's Thousand Best Churches* as "the best work in the county". Rotherham Minster, formerly known as Rotherham All Saints' Parish Church, is the third church to stand on this site. There was in all probability a church here before AD 937, and *Domesday Book* tells us that by AD 1086 Rotherham was an established settlement with its own mill, church and priest. Much of the present building dates from the fifteenth century, although there are parts remaining from the Saxon and Norman structures.

A walk away from All Saints' Church in Rotherham is the Bridge Chapel of Our Lady. With its parapets and pinnacles, it is a rare survivor of mediaeval times. Dating from 1483, it is situated on the original four-arched bridge over the River Don. There are only four surviving bridge or chantry chapels in England and Rotherham's is reputedly the finest example.

I remember in a history lesson being told that the retinue of the ill-fated Queen of Scots intended to break its long journey to Fotheringhay Castle at Rotherham but her regal group was stopped as it crossed the bridge. The worthy burghers of the town, in true Yorkshire fashion, refused her majesty entry when they discovered they had to pay for her board and lodging. She was sent on her way to Hardwick Hall in Derbyshire where she received greater hospitality.

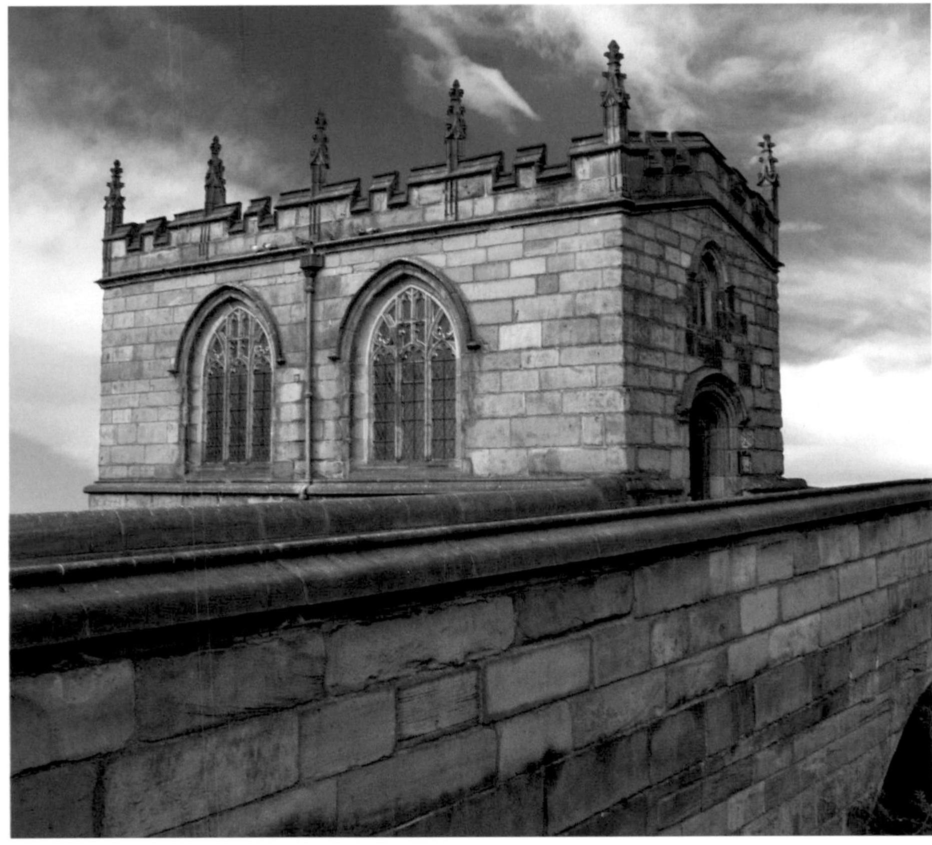

Tickhill, on the outskirts of Doncaster, was once one of England's most successful 'new towns'. Shortly after the Norman invasion, William the Conqueror granted all the lands around Tickhill to Roger de Busli, who built a motte-and-bailey castle on a small hill. Busli also co-founded nearby Roche Abbey.

The Guild of St Cross was established in the town and it is believed to have acted as the settlement's main governing body. St Leonard's Hospice (pictured right) was built in 1470 and can still be seen today.

The market cross in Tickhill (pictured right), known locally as the Buttercross, was built in 1777 by the Rev Christopher Alderson. It was erected in the market place in an attempt to revive the weekly market, but this ceased in the 1790s. A well-known annual event is the Christmas Eve carol singing which takes place at the Buttercross in the centre of Tickhill and is led by the Salvation Army band.

The Church of St Mary in Tickhill (pictured facing page opposite) is one of the very finest in the area. Pevsner, in his *The Buildings of England* series, describes it as "the proudest parish church in the West Riding, except for those of the big towns". It was built to replace the earlier church, All Hallows, as the settlement's principal church. St Mary's was already complete by the thirteenth century, indicating just how prosperous the community was at that time. Elaborate and extensive rebuilding took place over the century from about 1350 to 1450 when the nave and the tower were heightened to create the tall, light-filled building it is today.